Two Sides to Every Story?

An Examination of Ethics, Dilemmas, and Issues through Discussion, Writing, and Improvisation

Written by **Jonathan Gross**
Illustrations by **Jeff Richards**

©2012 Teaching and Learning Company, a Lorenz company

This book contains works of fiction. Names, characters, places, and incidents are the product of the author's imagination or are used fictitiously. Any resemblance to actual events, locales, or persons, living or dead, is coincidental.

The purchase of this book entitles teachers to make copies for use in their individual classrooms only. This book, or any part of it, may not be reproduced in any form for any other purposes without prior written permission from Teaching and Learning Company. It is strictly prohibited to reproduce any part of this book for an entire school or school district, or for commercial resale.

All rights reserved. Printed in the United States of America.

Teaching & Learning Company
a Lorenz company
P.O. Box 802, Dayton, OH 45401-0802
www.LorenzEducationalPress.com

Table of Contents

About This Book 3
The Chemistry of Love 4
A Kingdom of Conscience 10
To Tackle a Thief 16
Pizzeria Dreams 22
Charity 28
My Rival's Secret 34
Give the Gift of the Bristols 40
Gambling 46
Mr. Abbott 52
The Storm 58
The Bullied 64
A Sleepless Night 70
Fragile Truth 76
The Grime 82
One to Save 88

About This Book

Our lives are rife with difficult decisions and hard-earned lessons. It is easy to assign these experiences to the realm of adulthood when, in fact, we start dealing with them at a relatively early age. Perhaps it's the realization that we can cheat on a test, the question of whether or not to insult another person, or the struggle to choose between right and wrong when the lines are impossibly blurred. These experiences, and many others like them, are the foundations and first steps in building the characters that we eventually possess.

We have created this book with that knowledge in mind. Its 15 stories have been written to interest and entertain students. But more importantly, each story has been structured around an important lesson or a difficult decision. These aren't simple, by-the-book right versus wrong choices, either. The details surrounding each lesson or choice obscure an obvious choice with shades of gray, encouraging the child to sort through their own thoughts, opinions, and feelings before rendering a decision or determining the most important lesson.

Each story is supplemented with four unique follow-up lesson plans, each developing important skills. Discussion Questions challenge readers to rethink and analyze stories, emphasizing important lessons and introducing new perspectives. Role-Playing Variations give children an opportunity to express themselves creatively while interpreting and reflecting on their experiences with each story. Writing Suggestions develop language arts skills and deepen the value of each tale, pushing the student to create new stories of their own. Student Comments ask students to reflect upon deeper questions, applying the lessons learned from each story to their own lives and experiences, connecting them to the lessons and decisions in a new way.

The end result is 15 distinct units that challenge readers to look at life's often difficult decisions and lessons from multiple perspectives, allowing them to make more informed choices and observations. We hope that your students take these important skills and developments into their own lives and use them to better write their own stories across the pages of the world.

How to Use This Resource

The stories can be assigned for independent or small group reading. They can also be read aloud by either teacher or students. After finishing a story, use the Discussion Questions to get students talking. The questions don't need to be asked in any particular order. They should be a starting point from which students can direct the flow of conversation. Feel free to add your own questions and variations.

Each story's Role-Playing Variations offer improvisation activities of varying depth. These pages are written to the teacher, providing general guidelines for each activity. They can be assigned as is, or you can modify them to better suit the specific personality of your classroom.

Writing Suggestions can be assigned as homework or desk work. Encourage students to make each prompt their own. The suggested approaches are just that – suggestions. They are meant to get the student thinking creatively. The expression should be completely up to them. Again, feel free to modify existing prompts or to introduce your own.

And finally, the Student Comment pages are one-page essays that aim to deepen the student's connection with each story. These are 'big picture' questions designed to open up student perspectives, and to encourage application of lessons learned and decisions made to their personal experiences.

Note: It's important to explain to students that there are no right and wrong answers when it comes to this resource. They shouldn't hesitate to share their honest thoughts and opinions, even if their stance is morally or ethically controversial. When more points of view are expressed, discussion is greatly enriched.

The Chemistry of Love

The bell rings. Mr. Bink rises from his desk and shuffles to the bare podium perched in front of the desks. Bink stares out through thick lenses and down a wide nose, steel-gray eyes stern and acute. He begins his lecture.

Bryce watches the class visibly stiffen as Bink's high-pitched voice washes over them. One or two of the students giggled on the first day of class. The instant and extreme punishment that answered the laughter had quickly and clearly taught the first lesson – no one laughs at Bink.

Mr. Timothy R. Bink has been terrifying students at Hillock High for as long as anyone can remember. Universally considered the meanest teacher in the building, Bink is also known as the toughest. Advanced Placement Chemistry is no cakewalk to begin with. Add Bink and multiply by 23 unprepared students, and you have the compound for the most difficult class in history.

Bryce scored too low on the Chemistry entry exam and had to settle for College Preparatory Chemistry with Mrs. Stanton. But he exchanged one of two study halls for a position as Mr. Bink's teacher's aide. Why would he submit himself to such a woeful position? There are two reasons. Despite his nature, Mr. Bink was known to write college admissions recommendation letters for his aides. Bryce plans on attending college, and that recommendation would carry a lot of weight at Hillock State.

After a few moments of unsuccessfully trying to figure out the contents of Bink's lecture, Bryce turns his attention to the other reason for being in this room: Veronica Cameron. If Bink was the scariest thing about Hillock High, Veronica was the prettiest. With her long blonde hair, tan skin, and white teeth, she looked like a character plucked from a movie screen. Bryce had fallen for Veronica on the first day of high school, nearly four years ago. He had seen her coming down the hallway and time had slowed. Oh, he had fallen all right, and fallen hard. While staring at her electric smile, Bryce had walked directly into Hillock's impressively full trophy case. The impact knocked him out cold.

"Bryce!" Mr. Bink's squeal snaps Bryce from his daydream. All eyes, including the sky-blues of Veronica, are locked on Bryce. Despite the threat of severe reprimand, several smiles crack, unable to help themselves. Bryce feels his face flush a deep shade of red.

"I believe I assigned you several tasks to complete before the next bell," Bink continues. "I strongly suggest you begin. Unless you'd prefer to complete them in detention this afternoon?"

As Mr. Bink turns back to the class, Bryce drops his head. Had Veronica noticed that he was staring at her? Was she thinking about how big a dope he was right now?

Of course she isn't, Bryce thinks to himself. *She hasn't paid any attention to you in four years. Why start now?* Bryce had tried everything – secret notes slipped into her locker, flowers and candy grams on Valentine's Day; he'd even managed to get her phone number and send her an anonymous text message – which she'd never answered. Yes, he'd tried everything. Everything except actually walk up and talk to her, that is.

Bryce sighs as he opens Mr. Bink's grade book. *It's hopeless*, he thinks. *I'll never get a girl like Veronica to notice me. I'd have a better chance of passing AP Chemistry.* He begins transferring grades from the book to a laptop computer.

As his fingers fly over the keys, pecking the fate of each student into the system, Bryce keeps track of who is currently passing and who is failing. Far more pass than fail, he notes, but everything hinges on the final exam. The all-important test, which takes place next week, factors as 25 percent of the final grade. Everybody has a chance to make or break their Chemistry grade with the final exam.

A slight flutter roils Bryce's stomach when he sees Veronica's name. His fingers feel light and numb as he keys in the first few grades. He's so lost in thoughts of her that it takes him a moment to notice the grades blinking across the screen. They are shockingly low. He blinks twice and looks to the grade book to make sure he hasn't made a mistake. To his horror, he hasn't. He works and reworks the math in his head. If Veronica doesn't get an A on the final exam, she will *fail* AP Chemistry.

The bell rings. Students bolt for the door like racehorses out of the gate. Bryce watches Veronica's yellow backpack turn the corner into the hall and tries to swallow the lump in his throat. *Does she have any idea how much trouble she's in?*

"Did you complete the grade transfer?" Mr. Bink inquires from his desk. He opens a thermos and pours a cup of some foul-smelling soup.

"Yes sir." Bryce hastily enters the final numbers and saves the document. He gathers his things, hands the grade book and computer to Mr. Bink, and stumbles to the door in a haze.

"A moment, if you would." Bryce turns to regard Bink. "As you spent the first part of class in an idle state, I think I can borrow a few minutes of your lunch period for one last task, yes?"

It isn't a question. "Of course, Mr. Bink."

"Take this to the library and make me 23 copies." Bink shoves a stack of papers at Bryce. "If you aren't back in ten minutes, you will spend the rest of your lunch period removing gum from the bottom of my desks."

Bryce takes the papers and heads for the door. "Yes sir."

He is at the library before he realizes it. His mind is racing with the implications of Veronica's failure. He knows that she plans on going to Hillock State to play soccer. If she fails chemistry, she would have to stay another year! *She would be stuck here*, Bryce thinks. *And I'd be stuck at State without her.*

He punches the machine's keys and it begins spitting out copies. A future without Veronica is a future of horror. It would be like working as Mr. Bink's aide for a lifetime. The copier beeps and Bryce grabs the stack of warm paper. It's only then that he realizes what he's holding.

He is copying Mr. Bink's final exam. He's holding Veronica's salvation in his very hands.

I could take a copy. I could give it to Veronica. No, that's cheating. I could get in enormous trouble for doing something like that. What if Mr. Bink found out? No recommendation letter for me. I might even be expelled.

The library door opens. Bryce turns as Veronica walks into the room. As she slides past him on her way to a study table, her eyes meet his, just for an instant. His heart swells.

I'll never get a girl like Veronica to notice me. Until I do something worth noticing.

Point of View

Discussion Questions

1. What do you think Bryce will decide to do? How will he arrive at this choice? Will there be any negative consequences as a result? Positive consequences? Support your answers with details from the story.

2. What would you do in Bryce's position? Why?

3. Is there an honest way for Bryce to help Veronica? Come up with a plan in which he can still get her to notice him while honestly informing her of her risk of failing chemistry.

4. Have you ever been tempted to do something wrong for a good reason? What did you do? Explain your reasons for doing so.

5. Does love ever lead people to do bad things? Explain your answer.

Improvisation

Role-Playing Variations

1. Act out a scene in the library in which Bryce gives the test copy to Veronica. Let the students improvise dialogue and reactions. Give several students an opportunity to play the roles of Bryce and Veronica. Discuss the portrayals as a class.

2. Imagine that Bryce and Veronica are caught cheating. Act out a conference between Bryce, Veronica, and Mr. Bink. You might also include Bryce and Veronica's parents.

3. Have students deliver a short monologue in character as Mr. Bink. Encourage them to dress up in costume and create their own unique mannerisms for their portrayal.

4. Break students into pairs. Let them prepare and write a scene set three years after the events of the story. Bryce and Veronica are meeting for dinner. They discuss the events that unfolded in the library and after, and how they changed as a result. Let students decide such details as the nature of Bryce and Veronica's relationship, the choice Bryce made, and Veronica's final grade in chemistry.

Writing Suggestions

1. Write two lists: the pros of giving Veronica a copy of the test and the cons of doing so.

2. Write a short story from the perspective of Mr. Bink. What is this legendary teacher really like? What makes him tick? Does he enjoy his infamy or despise it?

3. The story mentions secret notes that Bryce put in Veronica's locker. Write one of these notes. Describe Bryce's emotions without revealing who he is.

4. Imagine that Bryce decides to copy the test and deliver it to Veronica. Write the library scene from her point of view. Establish how she feels about Bryce when he first approaches her. Does she know who he is? How do her feelings change after he reveals his plan? Does she go along with it? How does everything pan out for her and for Bryce?

5. Write an article for the school newspaper that covers the scandalous discovery of Bryce and Veronica's cheating scheme. Explain how they were caught and what punishment they will receive. Include interviews with the two students, along with Mr. Bink and other interesting individuals.

Name _____   Date _____

Student Comment

"Avoid a remedy that is worse than the disease."

This is taken from one of Aesop's fables. What does this moral mean to you? Apply it to everyday life. How does it apply to Bryce or Veronica in the story?

A Kingdom of Conscience

There once was a powerful king. His realm was vast and he ruled it with strength and kindness. His subjects were happy. They worked hard and the kingdom grew, until the time came when it could no longer fit comfortably within its borders.

So the king called a great council, assembling representatives from the people and the palace to discuss the future of their land. The people were happy, but they had no more room, they said. *Every piece of land is farmed, built upon, under water, or atop mountains*, explained an elderly farmer.

Does this cause my people difficulty? The king asked.

The people said no. They were never hungry, and their homes were safe and comfortable.

But the palace representatives grumbled. *We need more land*, a fat duke complained. *More land means more palaces. More palaces mean more farms to keep them fed. More farms mean more money for the kingdom's people.* Others nodded their heads in approval. *More!* They cried.

But there are other tribes beyond our kingdom's borders, a horse breeder's daughter pleaded. The king asked about these people. *They hunt and gather*, she explained, *and live in brightly colored tents. Each tribe has their own color, and together they look as a rainbow upon the land!*

The king listened to these things. He dismissed the council and retired to his private chamber. With him he brought his chief advisor, a close friend who had been by the king's side for many decades.

My kingdom is divided, the king fretted. *Half is happy, the other half desires more; which course is the wisest, old friend?*

Now, the chief advisor was a greedy man at heart. He was the secret voice behind those asking for more. He desired more property, wealth, and, above all, more power. *We must look to the kingdom's future, my lord*, he counseled. *We must ensure the prosperity of our children's children.*

But how, asked the king, *do we expand without upsetting the many-colored tribes of the rainbow?*

The chief advisor shrugged. *We are strong and powerful, my liege. If they resist our rule, we crush them like ants or scatter them like wind.*

The king frowned, seeing the wickedness and selfishness in his old friend's eyes. He stood up. *We shall not disturb these tribes. We shall be thankful for the wealth we already possess, and we shall preserve peace and happiness for our children's children. Thus shall their prosperity be ensured.*

The edict was delivered to the people, and they were happy. But the chief advisor seethed with rage and jealousy. He left the kingdom that very night, in secret, vanishing into obscurity.

*

Ten years passed, and the kingdom continued to flourish. The king married and had three children, whom he loved dearly. All was as it should be.

Then one day the great gong rang, warning of approaching danger. The king called the captains of his guard to discover what threatened his kingdom.

It is an army, the captains shouted, *come to conquer us! We are powerful, but our foes are too many. What shall we do, great king?*

I shall meet with this army's ruler, spoke the king. And he stepped onto a high balcony and watched the ranks of the enemy approach. They flew banners of many colors. The king recognized the very tribes he had spared ten years ago, united under a single banner of invasion. The army drew up at the palace gates.

Who leads this army against my peaceful kingdom? He shouted down. *Fetch me your commander, that I may bridge the gap between us and end this without violence.*

The leader stepped forward, clad in white armor, a gold crown beset with rainbow jewels upon his head. The king recognized the face beneath the crown. It was his old chief advisor and friend, returned from the past.

My old friend, the king asked, *why do you march against me?*

You foolish old man, the chief advisor sneered. *You denied me the power I craved. I am here to claim it as mine forever!*

Very well, the king began. *But I will not suffer violence against my subjects. What must I do to spare them any harm?*

You must leave, and surrender the kingdom to me! You must spend the rest of your life scratching a meager living outside this great kingdom's borders. What say you, the chief advisor asked.

The king considered at length. *I will do all that you ask*, he said, *if you grant me one wish. Let me take my family with me.*

You may take them, the chief advisor howled with triumph. *I shall require all of the palace for myself!*

Thank you, old friend. The king looked at the kingdom spread below him one last time and smiled, happy as could be. *Goodbye.*

*

People say that the old king took his wife and children into the countryside. They climbed a high mountain and found a hidden valley, rich with fresh water and fertile land. There they built a home and lived happily for all of the rest of their days.

The tribes saw the advisor's greed and lust for power plainly. They threw him into a dungeon cell and melted the key in a hot fire. They apologized to the people of the kingdom, and joined them to ensure a peaceful and prosperous future. The kingdom continues to thrive today, and it is not statues of the wicked chief advisor that stand in every plaza, but of the benevolent king who was always happy with what he had.

Point of View

Discussion Questions

1. Do you think the king made the best decision when he chose to leave the tribes alone? How would a different choice have altered the course of the story? Be specific.

2. If you were the king, what would you have done differently? Explain your reasons. Would your story have had a different ending than this one? What would that ending be?

3. Do you think this story could ever occur in real life? Why or why not? Can you think of any historical events that mirror this fictional one?

4. What lessons can we learn from the king? From the chief advisor? Provide details from the story to support your answers.

5. If you were one of the kingdom's citizens, how would you feel about each of the major developments in the story: the king's decision to leave the outlying tribes be; the invasion of the army under the old advisor; and the king's exile?

Improvisation

Role-Playing Variations

1. Choose several students to act out their own version of the council from the beginning of the story. What do the students advise their king to do? Does the king make a different decision? Let actors play their character as they wish, without restricting them to the story's arc.

2. Divide the class into pairs. Have each pair reenact the debate between the king and his chief advisor. The advisor should attempt to sway the king to taking the tribal lands beyond his kingdom, while the king should argue a course of peace and right action.

3. Split the class into several small groups. Each group should create a tribe to represent. They can create costumes, customs, and unique mannerisms. Once each group has created their tribe, role-play a scene in which the chief advisor comes to a gathering of tribes to persuade them to invade the kingdom. Let students improvise how the gathering and decision-making proceeds.

Writing Suggestions

1. Write an edict from the king to his people explaining his reasons for not invading the tribal lands outside the kingdom's borders. Use information from the story to establish the king's voice and explanations. Sign the edict with an appropriate name for this ruler.

2. Write the story of the chief advisor's betrayal. Define his character: give him a name, a back ground, unique characteristics, and a reason for going against his king's command. Focus on the events that transpire between the time he flees the kingdom and returns to conquer it, as well as his unfortunate end in a dungeon.

3. Write a description of the kingdom in which the story takes place. Settings to include are the capital city, the farmlands surrounding it, and the borders between the kingdom and the tribal lands.

4. Write a history of one of the tribes surrounding the kingdom. What is the tribe called? Where does it live? What is its society like? Its people? Does the tribe follow any unique customs or traditions – if so, how did they originate?

5. Write a journal entry from the perspective of one of the king's children. Describe the family's new life in exile. Where do they live? How do they survive? How do they manage to stay happy?

Name _____   Date _____

Student Comment

The king had everything a person could ever want: wealth, power, and loyal subjects. But he gladly gave it all up in an instant for the thing he held most dear: his family. Explain how this decision was so easy for the king, and why a character like the chief advisor would never understand it. What things in your life would you give up anything and everything for? Why?

_____
_____
_____
_____
_____
_____
_____
_____
_____
_____
_____
_____
_____
_____
_____
_____
_____
_____
_____
_____

To Tackle a Thief

After football practice, Clay and his friends always go to the large outdoor mall near school. They walk around, grab a bite to eat, and mingle with other students. It gives the tired athletes time to relax and recharge before they head home to study.

The spicy scent of pepperoni tickles Clay's nostrils and sets his stomach to rumbling. He begins to work his way towards the pizza place across the grass courtyard. They always greet Clay with smiles and give him the biggest piece. Normally, nothing stands between the bulky teenager and his meal, but today is different. The playoffs are in full swing, and the Eagles have a big game this Friday. Everyone in the courtyard stops Clay to offer their well-wishes and advice.

Clay smiles and takes it all in stride. Not only is he the best player on the field, he's the team captain, too. This is his job. Besides, he has to get used to the attention. Last month, he signed a commitment to play football at one of the best colleges in the country. Next season, the whole world will be watching him. So he spends a minute or two speaking with everybody on his way to the pizza place.

He is almost to the pizza stall when a strong hand grips his shoulder. Clay looks back to see Mr. Karl, a science teacher at the high school. He's also the father of Clay's best friend, Phil.

"Good practice today?" Mr. Karl grins. "You didn't beat up on Phil too badly, did you?"

Clay laughs. "Of course not. I wouldn't want to damage our friendship."

"I wouldn't want you damaging Phil," Mr. Karl chuckles. "Or yourself." His face falls into a serious stare. "You need to be sure you're taking care of yourself. One misstep could cost you that scholarship."

"Yes, sir." Clay has heard this same speech from countless others: his mom, his older brother, his coaches — even his tutors tell him to be careful.

"I mean it, Clayton. Pay attention on the field. That goes double off the field." A smile folds up Mr. Karl's face again. "No tree-climbing or skateboarding or other such nonsense." He pats Clay's shoulder for emphasis before moving off and into the crowd. His stomach protesting its emptiness, Clay makes a beeline for dinner.

As he waits for his extra-large slice of double sausage and cheese, Clay thinks about all the great things his scholarship means. He'll have a chance to fulfill his dream of playing professional football. He remembers tossing the ball around with his dad, all those years ago. His parents never complain about his utter devotion to the sport. They happily drive him to and from practice, attend games, and help him catch up on studying. If he ever makes it in the pros, he thinks, he will be sure to buy his parents a giant house and anything else they need to be comfortably taken care of for the rest of their lives. And, of course, the scholarship will get him out of this small town and out into the big wide world.

His pizza arrives. A young girl smiles as she hands it over. "Good luck this Friday. Go Eagles!" Clay smiles in response and begins to make his way back to his friends.

As he crosses the grass, he notices a commotion in the crowd. He squints in its direction, trying to make out the source of the noise and movement. Someone screams. A short, wiry man bursts out of the crowd, knocking down an elderly couple as he dashes towards Clay.

Clay is rooted in place, confused and shocked at the same time. The man bears down on him, moving quickly.

"Stop him," A woman's voice rises above the din. Clay thinks he might know the woman behind it. "He stole my purse!" He *does* know the voice. It's Mrs. Karl, Phil's mom!

Her purse is cradled in the thief's arm. He is halfway to Clay's position in the middle of the courtyard.

Cries answer the woman's plea from among the crowd. "Get him!" "There he is!"

Though many people are standing around, nobody makes a move towards the fleeing man. People cover their mouths in shock. Some point. Others turn and run away from the approaching figure.

"Clay! *Tackle* him!"

The last shout snaps Clay to attention. He looks beyond the thief to see Phil shouldering through the crowd, trying to give chase. He looks at Clay with helpless, pleading eyes.

He *should* tackle this criminal. Clay is at least double the man's size, and much more muscled. The guy's quick, but Clay knows that he is quicker. He nods at Phil.

He drops his uneaten pizza and turns to intercept the fleeing man. His muscles tense as he prepares to launch himself into the runner's path. Just before he springs into motion, though, something occurs to Clay: *the scholarship!*

What if he were to hurt himself attacking the thief? What if the man had a weapon or if there were more of them hiding in the groups of people? Clay hesitates. The assailant is just a few paces away. Clay imagines a broken leg, sees the scholarship letter torn to pieces. He sees himself coming to this same mall every weekend, unable to leave this town and fulfill his dreams. He envisions his parents struggling to make ends meet while paying his medical bills, and him never able to buy them that big dream house.

The purse snatcher looks into his eyes. He is close enough to touch. Clay realizes that he has to act *now*. And he does.

Discussion Questions

1. What *should* Clay do? Based on the story's presentation of his character, what do you think he *will* do? What would *you* do in his situation? Explain your answers.

2. Discuss the possible outcome of either decision. How could stopping or not stopping the thief have negative or positive effects?

3. Imagine Clay chooses not to intervene. Does this make him a coward? Does it make him sensible? Discuss reasons that validate his choice to let the thief escape unchallenged. How might the Karls react to this choice?

4. Is it a person's responsibility or duty to intervene in a situation such as Clay's? Explain your answer.

5. Clay's personal debate is between the present and future. If he challenges the thief, he might make the present situation better at the cost of his future. Conversely, if he lets the thief go, he makes the present worse while looking out for the future. Which is more important – the present or the future? Explain your reasons for choosing one or the other.

Improvisation

Role-Playing Variations

1. Act out the story as it is written. Assign students the roles of established characters, as well as several extras (crowd members). Give several students the opportunity to play the role of Clay. Each student should choose whether or not to intervene in the thief's escape. Let students improvise how that decision will change the ending of the story.

2. Clay steps into the thief's path and manages to stop the theft. However, he breaks his leg in the course of doing so. Break students into small groups. Have each group improvise a scene in which the Karls visit Clay at the hospital. What does Clay say to them? How does each member of the family react to Clay's actions? Discuss each portrayal as a whole class.

3. As a class, create a play in which a character has an opportunity to be a hero, though he or she knows that doing so will change their life in serious ways. Write a screenplay, assign and practice roles, and perform the play for parents or other students.

Writing Suggestions

1. Write a story that tells the events of this story from the thief's point of view. Who is he? Why is he stealing purses in the open? What does he think of this large person barring his way to freedom? Does he get away? Is he stopped? What happens to him in the end?

2. Write a newspaper article about the aftermath of the event at the mall. Base your facts upon your opinion of whether or not Clay decided to stop the thief. Include interviews with witnesses and persons of interest (the Karls, Clay, the football coach, etc.).

3. Write a letter from the college football coach for whom Clay is supposed to play, explaining that due to the injury he sustained stopping the thief, he will not be able to play football.

4. Write an entry in Clay's journal, set on the day of his last college football game. Reflect on the decision you made on that fateful day at the mall. Describe how it has made you a different person, and how it changed the way you lived your life during your days at college. Write about the next step – are you playing professional football next year? Going into law enforcement? Use your imagination.

Name _____   Date _____

Student Comment

Throughout history, individuals have sacrificed their own fortune and well-being in the name of a greater cause. This happens in big and small ways. Soldiers give their lives in defense of freedom in wars. Mothers and fathers give up their careers and free time to raise children. Why do you think people do this? What does it mean to sacrifice for the good of the future? How can you do this? List people and events you have experienced in your life that prove the existence of this phenomenon.

_____
_____
_____
_____
_____
_____
_____
_____
_____
_____
_____
_____
_____
_____
_____
_____
_____
_____
_____
_____

Pizzeria Dreams

The hour is well past midnight. The pizzeria is closed and quiet. Its upstairs office window, however, is still lit up. Inside, Cassie sits behind a desk, tapping away on a calculator. She has run the numbers again and again; things are bad. The pizzeria hasn't had a good year. The popular new pizza chain two blocks north has taken a lot of business from Cassie's modest diner.

Cassie's little corner eatery has never made her rich, but she has been able to pay all the bills and keep her loyal staff on the payroll. In recent months, she's made cuts, but she hasn't had to let any of her workers go. The numbers and figures on the desk before her tell her that that story will have to change. There isn't enough money to keep all of them employed and continue operating the pizzeria. In fact, there's only enough to keep half of them.

She thinks about her staff. Eddie and Saul; they were her first hires, almost twenty years ago. Both are past the normal age for retirement. They keep coming to work because they love it, but she knows that they need the money. Eddie's wife is sick; his pay goes to her medical bills. Saul supports his daughter, a single mother struggling to make ends meet. Regina, her best friend since high school, has been with the pizzeria since the very beginning. Mitch and Jasmine, the servers, had started by working summers. They had stayed on after they got married. They are putting two kids through school now.

She can only afford to keep one cook, but how can she choose between Eddie and Saul? There's no need for two servers, either. But the idea of firing one half of a married couple is hard to embrace. Hard as it is to admit, Regina's position isn't necessary. She helps out around the kitchen during busy times, and tidies the dining room and office; this work could be handled by the cook and server, or by Cassie herself. But a car accident two years ago had left Regina partially handicapped – how will she find another job in today's tough market?

Cassie pulls at her hair in frustration. She switches off the desk lamp and locks the office door on her way out. Her employees are more than workers – they're like family. How can she even think about letting any of them go?

As she climbs into her station wagon, a glint from the street's gutter catches her eye. Frowning, she bends down for a closer look. Nestled against the curb, in a pile of pebbles and dead grass, is a diamond ring.

She reaches down and picks up the ring. Its gold band is cold in her fingers. A diamond is set into the ring – an enormous diamond. Cassie peers up the street, cranes her neck around to look down it. There isn't a single person to be seen. With a grunt, she slips the ring into her jacket pocket and fires up the engine.

*

The next few days find Cassie's mood vastly improved. Business at the pizzeria is a little better than normal. A bout of warm weather improves everyone's mood, and the atmosphere is light and fun. Best of all, no one has come looking for the ring. She had been sure that someone would show up that next day, looking for their lost treasure. She expected every passerby to scan the sidewalk for the ring. But no one looked, and no one asked. The ring is locked away in the office safe. Yesterday, Cassie had taken the ring to a jeweler. He had cried out in appreciation when she revealed the ring. He said it was of the highest quality and craftsmanship. He doubted there were more than a handful of rings that could claim to be more magnificent in the entire world. When he had estimated its worth, Cassie's eyes had nearly popped out of their sockets – the figure was astronomical.

The longer the ring goes unclaimed, the more ideas run through Cassie's head. With just a fraction of the money the ring was worth, she could pay off the pizzeria and all of its equipment. She could buy all-new appliances and better ingredients – she could even lease a larger space and expand the operation. And best of all, she could easily afford to pay her workers. The future of her little pizzeria would be safe and secure. She finds herself wondering if this isn't a dream or a miracle.

Closing up the pizzeria one night, Cassie makes a decision. If she doesn't hear anything about the ring after two weeks, she will sell it to save her pizzeria and its workers.

*

The day has finally arrived. Cassie works through the lunch rush in a daze. She can't wipe the grin off of her face. After lunch, she removes the ring from the safe and slips it into her pocket. She has an appointment with the jeweler in 30 minutes. In less than an hour, she thinks, I'll be rich. And so will Eddie and Saul; Mitch and Jasmine; Regina. She descends the stairs, feeling lighter than air.

She walks into the dining room. Mitch is talking with a young man wearing an expensive suit. A beautiful girl in an equally expensive blue dress is standing at the front window, nervously chewing on a manicured nail. Cassie smiles at Mitch as she passes. But before she is through the door, he calls out to her.

"Cass? Before you go, could you help me out? This gentleman is looking for something – a ring. I told him we haven't seen any ring. I know it's a long shot, but you haven't found one, have you?"

Cassie's heart skips a beat. Her stomach rolls. She can feel the dream shattering around her. "A ring, you say?"

The well-dressed man steps up. "It's our engagement ring." He nods at the woman at the window. "And it's quite a rare and valuable piece. You'd certainly know it if you saw it. The diamond is simply massive. It's – well, it's very important to me. And to my fiancée, of course. Have you seen anything – anything at all?"

Cassie looks past the man, past his fiancée, out to the expensive sports car parked behind her old beat-up station wagon. She watches Jasmine wiping tables, hears Saul laughing at some joke Eddie tells in the kitchen. Regina is behind the counter, counting the register. Her family, working to keep her pizzeria running.

"Miss? Have you seen it? Have you seen my ring?"

Discussion Questions

1. Based on Cassie's character, what do you think she will do? What would you do in her place? Explain both answers.

2. What factors are motivating Cassie's decision the most? Are these the motivators that *should* be influencing her choice? Why or why not?

3. Imagine that Cassie decides to keep the ring. Do you think that she will come to regret her decision? How could such a choice backfire?

4. How do you think the employees of Cassie's pizzeria would feel if they knew about the ring? What would they advise?

5. Is it ever right to do something wrong in order to bring about something good? Be specific in your response.

6. Do you sympathize with the plight of the young, wealthy couple seeking their ring? Why or why not?

Improvisation

Role-Playing Variations

1. Break the class into small groups. Have each group act out the conclusion of the story and beyond, as they see it unfolding. Each group should perform their version of events for the entire class. Discuss each group's scene upon completion.

2. The story doesn't fully develop the characters that make up the pizzeria staff. Act out a typical afternoon at the pizza shop. Let students interpret the characters from the information in the story to portray their own version of these individuals.

3. Assume that Cassie keeps the ring and sells it to the jeweler. Act out a scene in which she tells her employees about the sudden wealth. How do they react? Do they ask questions? Do they remember the young couple looking for their expensive ring? How does Cassie respond to them? Conversely, set up a scene in which Cassie has given the ring back to the couple, and now has to lay off half of her staff.

4. The wealthy couple is suspicious of Cassie and asks an investigator to look into her. Break students into pairs – one to play the investigator and the other to play Cassie. Let the investigator improvise questions and Cassie answers.

Writing Suggestions

1. Pretend that Cassie kept the ring. Before she sells it to the jeweler, though, she has a change of heart. Write a letter to the engaged couple in which she admits to having the ring. Explain Cassie's reasons for lying, and how she arrived at the final decision not to sell the ring.

2. Write a story from the perspective of one of Cassie's employees. Describe their view on the financial situation of the pizzeria.

3. Write two lists: the first should be a list of pros for keeping the ring; the second should be a list of cons.

4. Write a newspaper article set one year after the events of the story. Focus on one of two topics: the surprising resurgence of Cassie's pizzeria or the closing of its doors. Detail how things have changed in the ensuing year and what has contributed to the business's rise or fall. Include quotes from Cassie and several of her employees.

5. Write a story about the young wealthy couple losing their ring, from the point of view of either the man or the woman. Are they really the snobs they appear to be? Does the ring have a story all its own? What do they do when they do or do not get the ring back?

Name _____ Date _____

Student Comment

Discuss the idea of the 'greater good.' What does this mean, exactly? How were Cassie's thoughts of keeping the ring in the interests of this 'greater good'? Compare this fictional situation to real-life issues that relate to this concept.

Charity

Maria was practically skipping through the mall parking lot. Excitement raced through her with every step. Just this morning, she'd received her very first paycheck from her summer job at the daycare. And she knew exactly what she wanted to do with the money. There was a sweet little boy at the daycare named Calvin. The two had become inseparable since they met on her first day. She played hide-and-seek with him every day, and he made different arts and crafts for her. His birthday was coming up, and Maria wanted to buy him something that he would love.

She was thinking about all of the cool gifts she could afford when she noticed the man approaching her from the other side of the parking lot. He was heading directly for her, his eyes locked on her. She looked away and tried to quicken her pace, but it was too late. Their paths would intersect in seconds.

The mall had always had a problem with beggars. Ever since Maria could remember, there had been men and women stationed around the various entrances, asking for cash or food. In recent years, the number had increased. Maria's parents always ignored them, pretending they weren't even there. She determined to use that tactic now.

"Excuse me, miss." Maria looked up to see the man blocking her path, arms held out in a half-shrug. She froze in her tracks, not sure what to do.

"I'm very sorry to bother you," the man began. Maria glanced at his clothes as he spoke. He was dressed in a faded tee shirt and jeans. His shoes weren't torn or dirty. He looked cleaner than many of the usual beggars. He didn't smell at all. His face, however, had the familiar weathered features. He looked as if he hadn't slept for days. He seemed drained of most emotion, a blank-faced robot.

"I've been out of work for four years and haven't been able to find a job since then. I lost my house last year and my wife can barely keep up with the payments on the new apartment. She's working two jobs…"

Maria found herself tuning out most of what he said. He rambled on, saying he saved every cent generous folks gave him for his son. If she could spare anything, anything at all, he would be eternally grateful…and on and on.

"Miss?" The man was staring at her, eyebrows raised inquisitively. "Please?"

"I'm sorry for your trouble, mister," Maria said with mock politeness. "I'm afraid I don't have any cash in my purse. I'd run to an ATM, but I have to be at work in a few minutes." She pointed at the mall to sell her story.

The man looked over his shoulder and back. He hesitated before stepping aside. "I'm sorry for keeping you, miss. Thank you."

*

Maria left the mall by a different exit, arms wrapped around Calvin's present. She'd spent most of her paycheck on it, but that was all right. She would get a new one next week and she could spend it on herself. She couldn't wait to see the look on Calvin's face when he opened up his gift.

She wound her way through rows of cars, keeping an eye out for beggars. They weren't all as quick to give up as that man had been. Some of them, her mother warned, might go to dangerous lengths to get what they wanted.

Her thoughts caused her to cry out in surprise when a figure stepped into her path from behind a van.

"Excuse me, m-" It was the same man. His eyes moved from Maria's face to the large bag in her arms. An expression of confusion flattened into a blank stare. "Excuse me." He stepped aside.

Her face burning red with embarrassment, Maria stalked to her car.

*

Calvin's eyes went big as the moon when he saw the gift Maria had given him. He jumped up and down with excitement and ran circles around the box. His reaction was worth every penny Maria had spent on the present.

"This is the best birthday ever! I'm gonna play with this *forever*!" Calvin was practically skipping as Maria walked him to the pickup area. She recognized the car his mother drove and angled towards it.

Calvin's mom was a sweet woman, and Maria couldn't wait to see what she thought of Calvin's new toy. She looked down at him as he hugged the box close to his chest.

He looked up and a smile lit his face. "Daddy!"

Maria glanced forward in surprise. She hadn't met Calvin's father before. He stood by the car, wearing a faded tee shirt and jeans, a clean pair of shoes on his feet. Maria stopped in her tracks as Calvin ran to meet him. It was him – the man from the mall parking lot. It was the same man, except now his face beamed with happiness and love.

"Daddy daddy daddy! Look what Miss Maria got me for my birthday!"

"Wow! That's so cool. What a wonderful friend. Did you say thank you?" He looked to Maria for the first time. His eyes widened in instant recognition. His smile faltered for a moment as he and Maria stared into one another's eyes. Calvin skipped around between them, happy as can be.

Maria had never felt so awkward in all her life. What must this man think of her? She was nervous and shaky. She worried that Calvin's father would be angry. She worried that he might tell the daycare's director about her shameful behavior at the mall. She desperately wanted to apologize. She wanted to make things right. But how could she? She looked into Calvin's father's eyes, desperate to find some kind of forgiveness in them.

Calvin's father broke the stare and looked down at his son. As Maria watched, the smile crept back onto his face. Then his lips broke into a wide grin. Her breath caught in her throat as she watched the transformation, relief flooding through her. He turned his beaming face back to her and opened his mouth to speak.

"Thank you, miss."

Discussion Questions

1. What is the most important lesson you can take from this story? Why is it so important?

2. What would you have done when the beggar approached you in the parking lot? Why would you have done so? How about the second encounter – what would you do then?

3. Did Maria do anything wrong? Explain your answer.

4. How do you think Calvin's father felt throughout the story? What do you think his initial opinion of Maria was? How did that opinion change when he saw her after shopping? In the daycare parking lot?

5. Have you ever been approached by a stranger asking for money or assistance? Discuss your feelings during and after the encounter. Do you wish that you had behaved differently after reading this story? Why or why not?

6. How would you react if you discovered that your mother or father was begging to help support you? Why would you feel this way? What would you do about it?

Improvisation

Role-Playing Variations

1. Give students a chance to change Maria's decisions in the story. Recreate the scene in which Calvin's father approaches her in the mall parking lot. Let each student perform their own version of what should have happened at that moment. Discuss the different responses as a class.

2. Create and act out a scene in which Calvin's father and mother discuss the events of this story, from the mall encounters to the daycare revelation, along with what they have learned from the experience.

3. Split the class into pairs and have them extend the end of the story. One student should play Maria; the second should play Calvin's father. They should improvise a discussion in which the two characters discuss the experience they have had. What have they learned? How have they changed? What will they do now?

4. Turn your classroom into a parking lot. Assign students random roles as shoppers and beggars. Let the students improvise a scene in which the beggars approach the shoppers and the shoppers react as they see fit. Afterwards, ask the beggars how they felt asking for help. Ask the shoppers how they felt being approached. Discuss how acting out these roles might change students' reactions to beggars in the future.

Writing Suggestions

1. Write a letter from an adult Calvin to Maria. Assume his father has explained the events of the story. What does he want to say to her?

2. Write a journal entry from Maria's point of view. What has she learned from her experience in the story? How will she use this knowledge in the future?

3. Could you ever beg? Write a one- or two-page response to this question. Explain what might drive you to do so, or what would keep you from doing it.

4. Write a newspaper opinion article about the importance of being charitable. Try to convince readers that they should give what they can whenever they can.

5. Write a story about a day in the life of a beggar or homeless person. Describe your character in detail – develop a history that explains how he or she got to this point. How do they fill their hours? What is their ambition?

Name _____   Date _____

Student Comment

Do those persons that live in elevated conditions (money, food and shelter, etc.) have a responsibility to help those who are less fortunate? How far does this responsibility go? How can you do your part to help those in need? Discuss the idea that we typically take our things for granted. How is this true? How can you change that mindset and daily appreciate the gifts you've been given?

_____
_____
_____
_____
_____
_____
_____
_____
_____
_____
_____
_____
_____
_____
_____
_____
_____
_____
_____
_____

My Rival's Secret

I used to be the most popular kid at school. I was the best soccer player in the city. I wore the coolest clothes. I had the most friends. Everything I did was a big deal. Nobody came close to my level of pure awesome; that is, until Tyson showed up this year.

I was holding court on the front steps, telling stories of my wild summer vacation, when, out of nowhere, this huge truck pulls up to the curb. I stuttered into silence mid-sentence, and everyone turned their heads to follow my staring eyes.

Out steps Tyson, wearing the latest designer jeans, a pair of trendy boots, and a bright yellow sweater I know for a fact I saw a Hollywood actor wearing in a summer movie. He surveyed the students gathered on the steps with bright eyes and a brilliant half-smile. Diamond studs in his ears complemented the shiny, obviously expensive necklace and watch he wore. His eyes flicked from face to face, until, at last, they met mine. They lingered on me for a half-second before dismissing me. I could feel how impressed the other kids were without even looking at them.

That morning was the beginning of the end for me. From the moment Tyson climbed the steps into our midst, my star began dimming. Tyson was a smooth talker, and by the end of the first week, he could be seen chatting up anyone and everyone. By the end of the first month, he was dating the prettiest girl in school. The other girls were mad with jealousy. He easily made the soccer team as backup striker – Coach was kind enough to keep me at starter. But I sprained my ankle in the first game, and Tyson has been starting ever since.

My fall quickened after that. By winter, I was an afterthought, just another kid following in Tyson's wake. Sure, I still had friends, but they all wanted to be Tyson's friends. I had cool clothes, but Tyson's were cooler. Nothing I did was that big of a deal; I couldn't come close to his level of pure awesome.

Even *I* was trying to be Tyson's friend. I said hello whenever he passed in the hall. I tried to pick his brain at practice. I tried to get a seat at his lunch table. But Tyson always looked at me as second-best, and didn't let me much closer than that.

In fact, he went out of his way to remind me that he was better. When I lost the starting job on the soccer team, I decided to run for class president. Lo and behold, as soon as I signed up, so did Tyson. You can guess who won. I was determined to lead the class in academics, but Tyson maintained perfect scores in every class. When I invited everyone to my annual Christmas break party, Tyson decided to throw his own party – on the same night. I spent the party drinking punch with my family while the rest of the class partied at Tyson's mansion across town. That was that. I was done. Finished. Over. From that night, I hated Tyson with every fiber of my being, and I vowed to do whatever I could to ruin him.

*

One cold morning in January, Tyson didn't show up for school. This wasn't that odd. He was known to get sick for two or three days at a time. I relished those short periods of freedom from his shadow. It didn't change anything; everyone still talked about Tyson. But he wasn't there to remind me how inferior I was. When he didn't show up at all that week, however, people started talking.

As vice president of the class, I was nominated (without any choice in the matter) to pay Tyson a visit, and take him a card signed by the entire class, imploring him to get better soon. Sick to my stomach, I walked to his parent's palatial estate after school. Several times, I thought of ripping the card into tiny pieces and scattering them to the wind, but I knew I'd just get in trouble, so I swallowed my pride and rang the doorbell. A young girl opened the door – Tyson's sister – and asked what I wanted. I explained the situation. She smiled and invited me into a massive hallway and asked me to wait while she fetched Tyson. I stared at all of the finery surrounding me. The house even smelled like money, I swear.

As I was waiting, the sound of raised voices caught my attention. Someone was yelling, and the other person was yelling back. I recognized the second person as Tyson. I crept towards the source of the voices and peered around a corner and into a large sitting room. Tyson was seated on a flowered couch, and an older version of him was standing above him, screaming down at Tyson. I guessed this must be his father.

He was really letting Tyson have it, telling him that he was a useless burden and a terrible son. I cracked a smile as I watched his humiliation. Never before had I ever seen Tyson treated badly.

My amusement snapped to horror when Tyson's father pulled his arm back and slapped Tyson across the face. I quickly stepped back around the corner, so as not to be seen, and retreated to the waiting area. I heard a few more sounds of violence from the sitting room and tried to ignore them.

A few minutes later, Tyson's sister appeared, the smile gone from her pale face. She explained that Tyson was still too ill to receive visitors. I handed her the card and left the house as quickly as possible.

As I walked home, I rethought my feelings about Tyson. He wasn't my favorite person, but no one deserved to be treated like that. Then it occurred to me – Tyson's frequent absences. Were they all because of his father's beatings? Rival or no, I had to talk to Tyson about what I'd seen.

*

Tyson finally came back to school yesterday, much to the students' relief. I finally got him alone after a student council meeting. I admitted what I'd seen at his house, and revealed my suspicions about why he missed so much school. I told him that he needed to talk to the principal, that he couldn't let this go on.

To my surprise, Tyson didn't agree or offer thanks. Instead, he got angry. He told me to mind my own business. He told me to leave him alone and stormed towards the door. Before he left, he turned around and told me that if anybody else found out about what I'd seen, that he would come after me. He promised that he would hurt me.

Now, I'm really angry at Tyson. I was just trying to be nice, to get him some help. He threw my kindness back in my face. Part of me feels like I should just forget it. If the kid wants to get beat up, so be it. But I know that's wrong. It's wrong for a parent to hurt their child, and whether he admits it or not, Tyson needs help. I can get him that help by telling someone. But what if Tyson comes after me, just like he said? What if he hurts me? What if he tells his father? What should I do?

Point of View

Discussion Questions

1. Step into the narrator's shoes. What would you do in his position? Give reasons to support your decision.

2. Is popularity important? Why or why not? Why do you think some people care so much about being popular or unpopular?

3. Discuss the reasons why it is absolutely necessary to tell someone about the kind of abuse Tyson is a victim of.

4. When the narrator confronted Tyson about the abuse, Tyson reacted very negatively. Why might someone in his position behave this way towards someone who is trying to help him?

5. How do you feel about the narrator of the story? Is he a sympathetic character? In what ways is he not a sympathetic character? Give details from the story to support your opinions.

6. Have you ever experienced feelings of envy towards someone? Why did you feel that way? How did you react to those feelings?

Improvisation

Role-Playing Variations

1. Act out key scenes from the story, such as Tyson's first arrival at school, the narrator's visit to Tyson's house, and the confrontation at the story's end. Allow students to create several original roles (classmates, for example) so that everybody can participate.

2. Have students write and act out scenes that are not included in the story. Let them create the setting, characters, and dialogue. Examples for potential scenes include: the soccer coach telling the narrator that Tyson will be the new starter; the student council elections; lunches in which the narrator tries to sit at Tyson's table; or the student council meeting in which the narrator is nominated to deliver a card to Tyson.

3. Divide the class into several small groups. Challenge each group to write their own version of what happens next. Does the narrator tell someone about Tyson's situation? Does he let the abuse continue? Does Tyson come after the narrator or have a change of heart? Let each group act out their conclusions for the rest of the class. Discuss the different ideas that the groups present as a class.

4. Hold 'auditions' for the roles of the narrator and Tyson. Give each student time to prepare a short performance that reflects their interpretation of the characters from the story. Allow each student to perform his or her narrator/Tyson for the class.

Writing Suggestions

1. The narrator is never given a name. Apart from his reflections on the story's events, we know very little about him. Create a character profile about him. What is his name? What is his family like? What made him into the character that exists in the story? What are his likes and dislikes, his hobbies and interests? Describe his physical features and mannerisms, as well.

2. Write an article for the school paper about Tyson's being elected student council president. Describe the details of the campaigns of both the narrator and Tyson. Compare their pros and cons as presidential candidates. Reflect on the impact that Tyson's election will have upon the school. Include student quotations about why they voted for either candidate.

3. Write a series of journal entries from Tyson's point of view. Start at the time of his arrival at school and continue through his rise to popularity. Finish with the day the narrator confronts him. Include Tyson's feelings towards the narrator as a classmate, his reflections on the abusive relationship between him and his father, and his plans for the future.

4. Write two speeches: one each for the narrator and Tyson. These are campaign speeches, delivered to the students of their school, detailing why each speaker should be elected as class president. Write each speech from the perspective of the characters you have come to understand from the story.

5. Write a letter to Tyson's father in which you reveal your knowledge of the abuse. Explain what you plan to do about it. Make clear your feelings towards him. Be certain that you maintain an ethical and appropriate tone throughout the letter.

Name _____   Date _____

Student Comment

Does your school have a popularity 'system' like the school in the story? Describe that system below. Which students benefit from it? Which do not benefit? What are the benefits? Discuss how such a system is wrong and bad for student development. What can you do to stop such behavior and put all students on an equal level?

_____
_____
_____
_____
_____
_____
_____
_____
_____
_____
_____
_____
_____
_____
_____
_____
_____
_____
_____
_____
_____

Give the Gift of the Bristols

Aaron looked up from his book when the music started. He knew the song well. It was the Bristols, his parents' favorite band. It was the song his father always played when he was sad. Quietly, he climbed out of bed and crept barefoot to the top of the stairs. He could hear his mother and father murmuring in the living room, but the music blocked out the words. He crept down to the landing.

His parents sat close together on the long couch. His mother's arm was slung gently about his father's shoulders. His father's head hung low. Aaron craned his neck over the railing to better listen for their words. Doing so caused the wooden boards beneath the carpet to squeak loudly. Aaron froze. His father's shoulders tensed; his mother turned her head. She smiled at him, but her eyes were wet with tears. She jerked her head in the sofa's direction. Aaron obeyed. He took a seat on the other side of his father.

After a few moments of nothing but the Bristols, Aaron's father explained. The factory had announced a new series of job cuts, and Aaron's father had been one of the victims. He had worked at the factory for almost 25 years. Aaron's grandfather had worked there until he retired. Most of his father's friends were factory employees. It was difficult news, and Aaron's father was taking it hard.

Aaron's mother tried her best to look at the bright side. *There are plenty of jobs for a well-trained worker like you*, she offered; *you'll be back at work in no time.* She winked at Aaron and he nodded vigorously, patting his father roughly on the knee. *No moping for my dad*, he told him. *He'll have a job before Christmas*! His father smiled weakly and agreed. A new Bristols song came on the stereo, and the family sang the lyrics together.

*

Three weeks passed. Snow fell in increasing amounts. Christmas was just ten days away. Aaron came in from an intense snowball fight and shook off his coat and boots. He ran into the kitchen, following the smell of his mother's famous spinach and cheese pasta. The Bristols were crooning about the joyous holiday season – his father was playing one of their Christmas albums.

As Aaron shoveled bowtie pasta into his mouth, Aaron's father cleared his throat, something he did before making one of his dinner table speeches. Aaron couldn't help himself. *You got a job*, he exclaimed.

Aaron's father frowned and opened his mouth to speak. *No, Aaron, I haven't been hired yet.* Aaron nearly choked on his spinach, feeling like a fool. *Your mother and I need to talk to you about Christmas*, his father continued. The Bristols belted out their rendition of *Rudolph.* Aaron's mother looked away.

Aaron's father explained that, because of his being laid off, the family didn't have much extra money that year. His mother was spending all of her income on bills. *I'm afraid we'll only be able to buy you one gift this Christmas*; his father tapped his fork on the table as he spoke. *And we'll have to stop paying you for chores for a little while.*

That's okay, dad, Aaron said. *I don't need lots of presents. And I've been saving my chore money for a while. I'll do my jobs for free*! Aaron's parents smiled at him. His mother hummed along with the Bristols.

*

Aaron stared at the pile of bills and coins on his desk. Shaking his head, he counted them again: 19 dollars and 78 cents. It wasn't enough to buy anything nice. It was three days before Christmas, and Aaron was starting to panic. He desperately wanted to buy his parents something that would make them forget their troubles, something that would make their Christmas better. But he had less than 20 dollars! He couldn't even buy them a nice dinner with that.

He sat back in his chair and thought harder. Maybe he could make them something useful. No, he thought, there's not enough time for that. He could buy them a really nice card or write them a sweet story. Not good enough! Frustrated, he switched on his computer and fired up the Internet. He opened Feeble and searched 'awesome cheap gift ideas.'

He scrolled through the first ten pages of results without any success. He moved the cursor to close the window before an advertisement caught his eye. 'Give the gift of music,' it said. 'Give the Bristols.' Aaron couldn't believe it. The Bristols had released a collection of their greatest hits! It was the perfect gift for his parents – it even included never-before-heard songs. He clicked on the link. When he saw the price, however, his heart sank. The collection cost 70 dollars. He would never be able to afford that.

Suddenly, a thought occurred to Aaron. His friend Nicolas had recently found a copy of the new Screamers album for free. He said he had downloaded it from a website called Tune Pirate. But there was a problem – downloading free music was illegal. It took money away from the bands and the companies that represented them. Nicolas had shrugged that detail off, saying that the bands were rich anyway – they hardly needed his money.

Aaron checked Tune Pirate for the new Bristols collection. It was available for download. All he had to do was click a button. He thought about how sad his father looked when he came back from an unsuccessful day of job hunting. He thought about how his mother cried when she thought no one was looking. He imagined their bright smiles when they opened the unexpected gift on Christmas morning.

But how would he explain the gift? What if they asked him where the money had come from? He couldn't lie to his parents. Would they be angry? Disappointed? Would they even notice? Aaron massaged his eyebrows in an attempt to clear his head. He stared at the 'Download Now' button on the screen and thought hard. Then he thought some more. Then he made a decision.

Point of View

Discussion Questions

1. Why is it illegal to 'pirate' (download without paying) music and movies from the Internet? Do you agree or disagree with the ethics behind this decision? Why or why not?

2. Does Aaron's situation justify his downloading the music for free? Explain your answer.

3. How do you think Aaron's parents will react to his gift? What details from the story make you feel this way?

4. Have you ever used websites like the one Aaron used in the story? Why did or didn't you do so?

5. What are some other gifts that Aaron could have given his parents without doing something illegal?

Role-Playing Variations

1. Conduct a talk-show interview with the Bristols. Students should create the characters that make up the band, as well as hosts for the talk show. The rest of the class should be assigned the roles of audience members who will ask questions and share ideas. The topic of the show is 'Pirating Music: Is It Wrong'?

2. Act out Christmas morning, assuming Aaron downloads the music and gives it to his parents. How do they react to his gift? How does Aaron respond?

3. Organize the class into two groups: one that is pro-pirating music and another that is anti-pirating. Give each group time to discuss and plan their arguments for their particular stance. Host a debate in which both sides present their arguments and discuss responses to them. Discuss the process and issue as an entire class. Be sure to explain that, ultimately, pirating is illegal and therefore wrong.

Writing Suggestions

1. Write a letter (from the point of view of the Bristols) to Aaron, explaining why he shouldn't pirate their music.

2. Pretend that you are Aaron. Write a fan letter to the Bristols, asking them for a free copy of their new CD. Explain your situation and your desire to not pirate their music.

3. Write song lyrics for the Bristols songs mentioned in the story. Give them titles, as well.

4. Write a biography of the Bristols. Include all members of the band, the instruments they play, their physical appearances, their personalities, and their histories. Describe where the band started out and how they rose to popularity.

5. Write a journal entry, dated Christmas, from the perspective of Aaron's father or mother. Describe receiving the gift from Aaron and realizing that it was illegally downloaded. How did they handle the situation?

Name _____   Date _____

Student Comment

Given their characters, if he gave them illegally downloaded music, Aaron's parents would likely teach him a lesson about the unimportance of material possessions. Why does modern society rely so much on possessions? Are possessions truly important? What is important? How can you focus more on the important things in your life?

_____
_____
_____
_____
_____
_____
_____
_____
_____
_____
_____
_____
_____
_____
_____
_____
_____
_____
_____
_____

Gambling

I've one friend in this wild world, and his name's Clancy. We was both born in tiny, dusty Stilltown. That is to say, it was tiny when Clancy and me was babies. You could say we grew up with the town. Nowadays, Stilltown's more of a tiny city, what with all the saloons, hotels, general stores, and, of course, casinos. Casinos – them what made the fortune of Stilltown and brought in all the people. But I'm getting off the path I was telling you about.

Clancy and me was fast friends. We did everything together. Clancy's ma passed on when he was just a baby, and his daddy went to work building railroad tracks a few years back. Ever since then, Clancy's lived with us, my very own brother and bestest friend. My daddy's the sheriff of Stilltown, and ma runs the historic Stilltown Inn. What with my folks being so busy, Clancy and me spend just about every minute together. We toss pebbles at prisoners through the jail's iron bars, break ponies at Stilltown Stables, and hunt snakes out on the plain when we ain't learning with Ms. Hendricks at the schoolhouse. Life has been right good to me and Clancy.

That is, life's been right good until just recently. Now, it's downright confusing. A couple months back, Clancy started disappearing every now and again. He'd vanish after school and crawl in through our bedroom window long after lights out. I kept asking him where he'd gone off to, but Clancy just told me to hush up and forget about it. One day, after school, I hid behind Graham's General Store and followed Clancy.

He led me down towards the river, and before long, we was in the heart of the Casino District. Now, I said that the casinos made Stilltown rich, and I spoke true enough. But like daddy says, with money sometimes comes bad men, and the casinos were full of such characters. Men with fancy suits and two six-shooters strapped to their waists. Drinkers and cheats. Desperate men that'd do just about anything to make a dollar. Daddy had forbidden Clancy and me to ever set foot in one of them casinos, but, sure as sunrise, that's just what Clancy did. He walked right up them steps and through them swinging doors, and he didn't come out until maybe four hours later, looking sad and tired.

Like I told you, Clancy's my own brother and best friend. I had to know what he was up to. So I hopped out from behind the barrel and about scared him out of his boots. I asked him what in tarnation he was doing in one of them casinos. Clancy told me to shut up and pushed past me.

I dogged him all the way back home. I stared holes through him at dinner and tapped my fingers on the wood desk as we practiced our sums. By the time we was settled in bed, he couldn't take it no more. He spilled that a few weeks back he'd taken to playing cards at the casino. He'd always seen the deputies playing at the jail and he wanted to try it. Problem is, you got to pay to play at the casino, and Clancy wasn't none too good at cards, being a beginner and all. So he lost his allowance playing. But he thought he could get better, so he kept going back. Only he didn't get no better. Last week, Clancy had borrowed money from a 'friend' at the casino and lost it all. Another 'friend' had given him money so that Clancy could win the first man's money back. Except he lost the second friend's dollars, too. You can guess how the rest went. Clancy was in deep with more than a few gentlemen and lesser folk down at the casino, and he didn't rightly know how he was going to dig himself out of this hole.

Well, it seemed pretty simple to me, I said. Clancy needed to talk to pa. The sheriff would take care of the money he owed, so long as Clancy promised to pay pack what he owed. And Clancy could never again set foot in the Casino District.

But Clancy was having none of that plan. He knew what father thought of the casinos, of the men and women that spent their hours within them. He didn't want pa to think the same of him, nor experience the punishment the sheriff would certainly lay upon him. Besides, Clancy said, I love playing cards. I'm getting better. And my friends at the casino gave me time to pay 'em back. Just you wait. Before you know it, I'll have enough money to stop burdening your folks. I'll buy myself a plot of land and make my own fortune, and you and me will have horses and six-shooters and fine suits and hats.

Clancy's eyes went all big and round when he said it, and I confess I didn't have the heart to argue with him. I told him I'd keep my mouth shut, so long as he promised not to borrow any more money.

The next night, after Clancy thought I was sleeping, he snuck out our window. I followed the rascal. Down to the Casino District we walked, but Clancy didn't walk into no casino. Instead, he walked into a large yellow-painted saloon. A saloon every man and woman with a brain in their head knew, and any man and woman with any sense in that brain knew to stay away from – Rafferty's.

You see, Rafferty is the dirtiest crook in all of Stilltown. Daddy had been trying to put him in jail for years. He used to rob stagecoaches out on the plains, until he came to town and opened his saloon, where all manner of illegal services could be arranged: murders, robberies, gambling loans, and believe me nobody wants to know what else. Which was my guess as to why Clancy was inside the den of evil. The thing about Rafferty's loans, however, was this: when they weren't paid back on time, real bad things happened to the man that owed. Unspeakable things.

So I seen Clancy walk in, and a half-hour later, out he comes with a heavier jacket, heading for the nearest casino with a confident step. I couldn't help myself, I ran into the casino after him and grabbed Clancy's arm. I begged him to take the money straight back to Rafferty. I'd give him all the money I had saved, and together we would pay back the men he owed money to. He had time, after all.

Clancy pulled me into a dark corner and told me that he'd lied, that the men he borrowed from weren't nice and they hadn't given him no extra time to return their money. It was now or never. I pleaded with Clancy to come back home and tell his story to daddy. Clancy told me he wouldn't involve my family. He said it could be dangerous for ma and pa, with Rafferty involved, and he wouldn't see them or me threatened. This was his problem and he needed to solve it on his own. He made me promise to leave it alone and go home. Clancy's my bestest and only friend, so I did just that.

Clancy's in the casino right now, gambling for his very life. Last I heard, he's winning. Of course, your luck can change in an instant when it comes to cards. I don't know what I should do. If I tell my daddy and he gets involved, things might get ugly. Rafferty isn't a man to mess with, even for the sheriff. Plus, I'd be breaking my promise to Clancy, and he wouldn't want to speak with me no more. He'd probably leave the house and strike out on his own, and I don't know where he would go or how he would survive. If I don't tell daddy, and Clancy's luck goes sour, there's no telling what will happen to him. I'm in a pickle here. What should I do?

Point of View

Discussion Questions

1. What should the narrator do? If you were in his shoes, would you go along with Clancy's plan? Would you tell the sheriff? Are there additional solutions that the narrator hasn't considered? Give detailed reasons to support your answers.

2. Given what you understand about the narrator from the story, why might he choose to keep Clancy's problems a secret? How might he justify this action?

3. Gambling continues to be a popular element of modern entertainment. Is gambling wrong? Why or why not?

4. How have ideas of right and wrong changed since the time of the Wild West? Is the world a better place? Include specific examples in your response.

5. What would you do if your best friend (or a family member) started gambling? Would you confront him or her? How would you go about it? How might they respond to your intervention?

Improvisation

Role-Playing Variations

1. Act out the story as it's written. Write dialogue for key scenes, such as the narrator's confrontations of Clancy. Or you might allow students to improvise lines, instead.

2. Have students act out key scenes not present within the story. Examples might include Clancy's meeting with Rafferty, Clancy's experiences with money-lenders at the casino, or the narrator's revelation of Clancy's situation to the sheriff.

3. Form your class into several small groups. Explain that each group must create an ending scene for the story. Groups should assign roles to each member, write out a basic screenplay, and act out their scene for the rest of the class. Discuss the different endings as a class.

4. Imagine that the narrator tells the sheriff about Clancy's dealings with Rafferty. Consequently, the sheriff arrests Rafferty on multiple charges. As a class, act out Rafferty's trial and sentencing. Include testimonies from Clancy, the narrator, and the narrator's parents, as well as several student-created characters. Try to create a role for each student.

5. Two panels of Stilltown citizens come before the town council to debate the casinos and the issue of gambling. One is pro-casino; the second is anti-casino. Set up three groups: the town councilors, the pro-casino petitioners, and the anti-casino petitioners. Act out the debate, allowing each group time to make their case. Let the town council consider both sides before rendering their verdict. After the role-play, discuss the debate and the implications of its outcome.

Writing Suggestions

1. Write a letter from a concerned casino owner to the sheriff of Stilltown. You are concerned that your casino is playing host to less-than-moral activity. But you believe in the integrity of your casino as a money-making Stilltown business. Try to convince the sheriff to look favorably on your operation, and provide suggestions for how to limit illegal or amoral activities, such as money-lending.

2. Adapt this story for modern times. Create a new cast of characters, an alternate setting, and apply the story's themes and dilemmas to the world of today.

3. Write a newspaper article about the casino district of Stilltown. Include details about how the district has changed the town (for good and ill). Conclude the article with your verdict on the casinos – are they good or bad for Stilltown?

4. Write two journal entries, one each from the narrator's and Clancy's points of view. Set the entries ten years after the events of the story. Describe what each character is doing with their life, and how their experiences with gambling and the casino changed them. Here are some possible questions to consider: Are they living in Stilltown? Are they still best friends? How do they make their livings? Is there still a casino district in Stilltown? Use your imagination and include unique pieces of information from each character.

5. Write a scene of dialogue between the narrator's mother and a Stilltown Inn guest, discussing the issue of gambling. Imagine that the narrator's mother is adamantly against it, while the guest is in favor of its practice.

TLC10596

Name _____ Date _____

Student Comment

How important is friendship to you? The story's narrator struggles with the decision to do what Clancy wants or what he feels he should do. Would you ever do something 'wrong' in order to help a friend? How far would you go?

Mr. Abbott

Brooke takes a sip of cool sweet lemonade before settling back in her folding chair. She and her friends are lounging by the pool in her backyard, soaking up the hot July sunshine. Pop music blares from the radio. Cherise and Maggie are splashing and laughing in the water, Jen and Kim are gossiping. All things considered, it is a perfect summer day. She closes her eyes and breathes a long satisfied sigh.

"Turn off that awful noisy filth!" A voice like crumpled paper startles Brooke. She sits up and sees a wrinkled face peppered with gray and white stubble frowning at her from across the fence. Mr. Abbott, her awful neighbor. Dark eyes glare at her through silver-rimmed spectacles. His lips twist in a sneer and his yellow teeth gnash together. "I can't hear myself think for all that racket. And put on some proper clothes! Those 'swimsuits' are far too revealing! What would your mother think?"

Mr. Abbott has been terrorizing Brooke for years, ever since she can remember. She is always being too loud or disrespectful, trespassing on his property or disturbing his rest. And he is always quick to tell her so. One of Brooke's earliest memories is toddling into Mr. Abbott's garden and wailing at the tongue-lashing she got for it.

She stands up from her chair, irked by the interruption. She strides over to the radio and twists the volume knob counter-clockwise, lowering the peppy tunes a fraction. She glances over to the fence, where Mr. Abbott *harrumphs* his approval. He turns and begins to shuffle back to his house. When she sees his back, Brooke cranks the knob clockwise. The quiet song flares higher into the afternoon. Mr. Abbot snaps his head around, rage darkening his features. Brooke offers him an indifferent shrug and saunters back to her chair, her friends squealing with laughter.

Several minutes later, Brooke's mother appears on the pool's deck. She beckons with a finger. Brooke follows her until they are out of the girls' earshot. A heated exchange follows, ending with Brooke's mother telling her in no uncertain terms to turn the music off or send her friends home. Reluctantly, Brooke returns to the pool and switches the radio off. She flops into her chair and huffs a long frustrated sigh. Across the fence, she catches Mr. Abbott frowning triumphantly from a back window.

*

That evening, Brooke helps her mother dry the dishes. She spends much of the time complaining about Mr. Abbott. "He's always upset about something. I can't help it that I'm not old and cranky and always in a bad mood."

Brooke's mother sighs and dries her hands. "Brooke, honey, sit down. I want to tell you a story about Mr. Abbott."

Brooke frowns and sits down at the kitchen table. "Fine. But hurry up. The girls are coming over in an hour."

When she and Brooke's father first moved to the neighborhood, her mother explains, Mr. Abbott had been living next door for several years. He was a different man then, and had lived a different kind of life. His wife was still alive, and their two grown children were over for dinner every Friday night. Brooke's mother and father attended some of these dinners. Mr. Abbott had been bright-eyed and playful, quick to tell a joke and even quicker to compliment his new neighbors. He and Brooke's father would often meet at the back fence and share stories of cars and sports and travel. Many were the times, Brooke's mother smiles, when I went to sleep while your father listened to one of Mr. Abbott's gripping war tales late into the night.

Just before Brooke was born, she continues, Mr. Abbott's wife grew very ill. Doctors told her that she didn't have long to live. Mr. Abbott was convinced that she would get better, despite the odds. He set up a special sickroom in the house, sparing no expense. He retired from his job at the local electricity company to attend to her every need. She held on for longer than expected, but it couldn't be helped. When Brooke was still a baby, Mrs. Abbott passed away.

Mr. Abbott was never the same. He came outside less and less. When they did see him, he was withdrawn. His children stopped showing up for dinner. Brooke's father even saw Mr. Abbott screaming at them one afternoon. After that, they stopped showing up at all. Before long, any attempt to speak to Mr. Abbott was met with a frown and unkind words. Brooke's parents gave up trying to lure him out of his grief, hoping he would find his way back to his old self. That was years ago, Brooke's mother concludes.

There is a knock at the door. "That's probably the girls." Brooke stands up.

"The next time you think about being rude to Mr. Abbott, try to remember how he used to be." Brooke's mother folds her arms over her chest. "Try to imagine how difficult losing a loved one would be."

*

Hours later, the girls huddle beneath the bushes dividing Brooke's yard from Mr. Abbott's. Jen and Maggie open a duffel bag, revealing several rolls of toilet paper, bright white in the moonlight. The girls grin at one another in the darkness.

"This will give the old man plenty of time to hear himself think." Kim giggles. "It'll take him days to clean all this up."

"I'd like to watch him try to climb a ladder to pick it out of the treetops." Cherise snorts with glee. She reaches into the bag and distributes the rolls among the girls.

Brooke watches as the other girls crawl around the bushes and spread out. They begin festooning tree branches with long strands of paper, stifling laughter as they work. She starts forward but hesitates, glancing back at her house, then at Mr. Abbott's upstairs window.

Jen's face pops up over the bushes. "What are you waiting for, Brooke? You should be the one throwing the most. You have to live next to the old fossil." She smiles mischievously.

Brooke doesn't say a word. She drops her armload of paper and goes home.

*

The following morning, Mr. Abbott wakes up before the sun rises. He looks at his nightstand, surveying the war medals and commendations. He looks over the photographs of his two children. His eyes linger on the picture of his beloved wife. He slowly rises from his bed and slips on a worn brown robe. He descends the stairs and starts a pot of coffee in the kitchen. He walks out onto the front porch to retrieve the daily newspaper. As he bends to pick it up, something catches his eye. He reaches out and plucks a wispy white strand of paper from the rose bushes bordering his porch. He inspects it closely. He surveys the front yard – everything is in order. He shrugs and turns to go back inside. He sees his neighbor's porch, where the rude girl from yesterday rests on a porch swing, fast asleep, two bulging garbage bags at her feet. He frowns a confused little frown, *harrumphs*, and goes back inside.

Discussion Questions

1. What does the story imply that Brooke did? Why do you think she did this? Would you have done something different? Explain the reasons for your decision.

2. How do you feel about the character of Mr. Abbott? Do you like or dislike him? Why? Does Brooke's mother's story change your feelings at all? Why or why not?

3. Why did Brooke let her friends toilet paper the house and then clean it up alone afterwards? Why didn't she just stop them? Or blame the incident on them the following day?

4. Have you ever taken part in any sort of prank? If so, why did you do it? Do you regret your actions? If you haven't, would you ever consider doing so?

5. Brooke's parents gave up trying to coax Mr. Abbott out of his state of bitter solitude. How could they, and Brooke with them, continue to reach out to him, despite his nature?

Improvisation

Role-Playing Variations

1. Reenact the first scene of the story. Give all students a chance to portray Mr. Abbott. Encourage them to put their own spin on his over-the-top personality. Let other students portray the girls, improvising unique reactions to each of Mr. Abbott's portrayals.

2. Next, give the students a chance to play the role of Mr. Abbott as told by Brooke's mother. Stage a dinner scene in which the Abbotts and Brooke's parents interact. Let students improvise topics of discussion and character lines. As a class, discuss the differences between the two styles of Mr. Abbott.

3. Choose one student to play Mr. Abbott. Send him or her out of the room; the actor should return in exactly five minutes. 'Toilet paper' the classroom with the rest of the class. Drape rolls of toilet paper over desks and chairs. Make sure you are still in the act when Mr. Abbott returns to the classroom. The actor should react to the scene he or she walks into (as Mr. Abbott). Let students try to explain themselves or escape the situation.

4. Imagine that Brooke isn't able to complete her cleanup before Mr. Abbott awakes. Divide the class into pairs and let them improvise a scene in which Mr. Abbott confronts Brooke, while she tries to explain the situation. Pairs should perform their scenes for the rest of the class.

Writing Suggestions

1. Write a story in which you move to a new home and discover that Mr. Abbott is your neighbor. Include a confrontation between yourself and your new cranky friend. How do you react to him? Bring the story to a clear conclusion that describes your plan.

2. Write three journal entries as the character of Mr. Abbott. The first should be set in the past, when his wife was healthy and his outlook on life positive. The second should be after his wife's death, as he struggles to deal with his loss. The third should be from the day the story ends, after he witnesses Brooke sleeping on her porch.

3. Write a description of the late Mrs. Abbott. What did she look like? What was her personality? Did she have any hobbies or favorite things? Portray a complete character.

4. Write an alternate ending for the story, assuming that Brooke goes along with the scheme to toilet paper Mr. Abbott's house. What happens? How does Mr. Abbott react upon discovering the mess? How does Brooke feel upon witnessing this reaction? Is she found out?

5. Write a story about a prank gone horribly wrong. Include several characters, the details of the prank, and details on how things went awry. Conclude with the consequences of the story's events.

Name _____ Date _____

Student Comment

"Respect your elders."   "Try to walk a mile in his shoes."

Choose one of these adages and explain its meaning. How does the story include the spirit of this piece of wisdom or advice? Discuss examples of it from your own life. How can you learn from these words and apply them in daily living?

The Storm

The rain started at dusk, light at first, a sweep of chilly drops blanketing the flat landscape. Nathan McReedy glanced over his shoulder, through the loft's wide opening. A flicker of lightning bolted to earth in the distance. A gentle peal of thunder followed, rolling over the land like a warning.

"Are you gonna go or what?"

Nathan turned back to the barn's interior. He walked slowly to the loft's edge, gazing down to the first level. Sprawled atop a thick pile of hay was Taylor Deters, his longtime playmate and best friend. His copper hair fell in thick curls across one eye. He flicked them back with a slender hand, revealing a freckled face. His green eyes flashed mischief as he smiled lazily.

"Well?" Taylor asked.

"I'd be ready to do it, if you weren't in my way." Nathan grabbed a fistful of feed from an open sack and showered it down on his friend. Taylor held a hand in front of his face and lifted his long limbs from the pile.

"It's all yours, high flyer," he said as he leaned against a stall door, one leather-booted foot propped behind him.

Nathan took a deep breath and took a few backwards steps. Ordinarily, he and Taylor would never get away with a stunt like this. His younger sister Ginny would have told Mom and Pop straightaway, and that would be that. But Ginny was gone, and Mom and Pop with her, on a weekend visit to Uncle Cam's. Nathan was supposed to be working on his science report, but, well – that was that.

A crack of thunder, much closer now, startled him from his thoughts. He could just see Taylor's head from his vantage point. His friend was frowning up at him, as if to say, *What are you waiting for?* He took a deep breath and held it.

He nodded to himself and broke into a run. His steps *thunked* across the wooden floorboards. His right foot hit the edge of the loft. He channeled all his energy into that foot and sprang with all his might. Then he was in the air, suspended like a drop of rain in the stormy sky. He took it all in, the horses eying his flight suspiciously, the suspended lights swaying like mad in the wind coming through the double doors, Taylor's admiring expression as he watched his friend soar above it all.

Then, without warning, he was falling, plummeting towards the hard packed dirt floor with incredible speed. A frightened croak began somewhere deep in his chest, but the hay was coming at him too quickly to give it voice. He didn't even have time to close his eyes.

WHUMP!

Nathan was face down in the hay pile, rough stalks tangled in his hair, poking through his thin shirt. He was alive. He clutched a tuft of the saving stuff in each hand and flopped onto his back, launching the hay into the air with an ecstatic cry.

"Not bad," came Taylor's voice. He was already climbing the ladder to the loft. "You looked like one of the earliest planes." He laughed over his shoulder. "One of the ones that didn't work, that is."

He reached the top and spun around, arms spread theatrically. "Lemme show you how to fly!" The rain was falling hard now, hundreds of drops slamming on the barn's roof. Taylor backed up and out of Nathan's sight. A full-throated yell sent Nathan scrambling out of the hay pile. A moment later, he heard Taylor start to run.

He leaned against a support and waited for the show. Taylor was moving fast, eyes wide with excitement and anticipation. He would make this a good jump, Nathan was sure of it.

A loud crack issued as Taylor approached the edge. A floorboard splintered under the boy's weight, shreds of wood cascading to the ground. Taylor's eyes grew wider still as his left leg sank into the gap to his shin. Only he didn't stop – he was moving too fast. He folded into an awkward somersault, screaming as his leg was wrenched from the hole in the floor. He flopped over the loft's edge, arms flailing. He rolled over in the air before landing a good distance from the hay pile. His knees hit first with a sickening crunch, and Taylor pitched forward, head smacking the ground. He lay unmoving as Nathan vaulted to his side.

He shouted Taylor's name, shook his body by the shoulder, poked him over and over. Taylor rolled with the movement but did not wake up. Nathan noticed a deep cut on his shin, bleeding badly. He didn't know much about injuries, but he knew enough to see this was a serious one. He put his ear to Taylor's chest and felt the gentle rise and fall of his breathing. He had to do something. He had to get help. He had to call 911. He didn't have a cell phone – Pop said he could buy one when he got an A in science – but Taylor did! He patted Taylor's pockets until he found the shape, reached in and pulled out a cracked and broken phone. It would have to be the house phone then.

He rose and raced towards the barn entrance, saw the driving rain outside. He couldn't even see the house's lights through the haze. A flash of lightning illuminated a shape just outside the barn – Grandpa's old pickup truck, rusted and dented all over from hard use.

Nathan hesitated. He knew the keys were in the glove box. The truck, while old, was in decent condition. Pop took it into town from time to time. He looked back to Taylor, lying on the ground. He looked paler. Nathan thought hard. By the time he got inside, dialed 911, and explained the situation, he could have Taylor in the cab and be on his way to the town hospital. It wasn't far, and he knew the way.

There was only one problem – Nathan was only thirteen years old! He'd never driven a car before. Pop wouldn't even let him run the farm's tractor, let alone Grandpa's truck. Once, Taylor had driven his brother's car to the McReedy's farm from town. Mom had gone crazy with anger and worry, and Pop had been worse. His parents had forbidden him to go near a car until he was old enough to get a license.

But he'd watched his parents drive a thousand times. Gas pedal, brake pedal, steering wheel – that's all there was to it, right? Surely he could make it the two miles to the hospital. It was getting late, and he knew the roads would be almost empty. Still, something held him back, kept him standing in the barn's doorway, drops of rain blowing onto his skin and making him shiver. A brilliant flash of lightning touched down dangerously close to the farm. Behind him, Taylor moaned softly. He had lost a lot of blood.

Whatever he did, Nathan had to do it now. Another minute of debate could cost him the chance to save his best friend. He looked through the storm to his house a hundred yards away, from the house to the old rusty pickup. He looked at Taylor. Finally, he looked to his own hands, trembling slightly from the rain's chill. He balled them into fists of frustration. He didn't know what he should do.

TLC10596

Point of View

Discussion Questions

1. Based on what the story reveals about Nathan, what do you think he will do? Why? Provide specific details from the story to support your answer.

2. What do you think Nathan should do – drive Taylor to the hospital or call and wait for help? Explain the reasons behind your opinion.

3. Why is unlicensed driving such a serious crime? Why do you think some people choose to ignore the law? How might organizations emphasize the importance of not driving without a license?

4. Describe a situation in which your emotions conflicted with something you were supposed to do. How did you react? Would you respond differently now? Explain your answers.

Improvisation

Role-Playing Variations

1. Choose students to play the roles of Nathan and Taylor. Act out the story as it's written, but continue through Nathan's decision. Let each pair of students improvise their own ending. After you've enacted the story several times, discuss the different conclusions as a class.

2. Divide the class into groups of three. One student should portray Nathan and the others his parents. Let students improvise discussions about the incident with Taylor. Nathan's parents should ask questions that cause him to explain the reasoning behind his choice (whatever the students decide it is).

3. Imagine that Nathan decides to drive Taylor to the hospital. Later, he is interviewed by a police officer. Step into the role of that officer. You have reviewed the circumstances of the event, and you have several tough questions for Nathan McReedy. Explain to the class that each student should portray Nathan. Ask random students your questions and let them improvise responses.

4. Let student groups create and act out scenes in which the law and ethics or morality come into conflict (for example, a mother stealing food because she can't afford to feed her children). They should write the characters, setting, events, and dialogue. Let each group act out their scene for the entire class. Discuss the unique considerations and complications of each one as a class.

Writing Suggestions

1. Write an ending for the story. How badly is Taylor hurt? Does he get to the hospital in time? How does he get there? What consequences, if any, result from Nathan's decisions?

2. Write a journal entry from Taylor's point of view. Assume he made it to the hospital in time and makes a full recovery, thanks to Nathan's actions. How does Taylor feel about the incident? How does he plan on thanking Nathan? Did this event change his life? How?

3. Make a list of positive and negative consequences that could result from Nathan driving Taylor to the hospital. After reviewing your lists, write a one-page argument for one side. Include at least three reasons to strengthen your argument.

4. Ten years have passed. Nathan and Taylor run into one another. Write the ensuing conversation. How have they changed in the last decade? Are they still close? How did the fall and its aftermath shape the next decade of their lives.

5. Write a newspaper article about Nathan saving Taylor's life. Describe his actions. Include interviews with Nathan, Taylor, and Nathan's parents. How is law enforcement responding to Nathan's illegal driving?

Name _____ Date _____

Student Comment

In the story, Nathan struggles with doing what he legally should and what he feels he rightly should. What is the difference between *right* and *legal*? Which is more important? Why? How might what is right and what is legal come into conflict? Describe and reflect upon any personal experiences with this issue.

_____
_____
_____
_____
_____
_____
_____
_____
_____
_____
_____
_____
_____
_____
_____
_____
_____
_____
_____
_____

The Bullied

I'm late! Darius tore down the sidewalk, slinging up snow with each step. Houses whizzed by and a cold breeze numbed his cheeks. As he churned by the church, the eight o'clock bells clanged their first note. *The bells are five minutes ahead of school clocks. I can make it!*

He rounded a corner and the school came into view. His legs burned and his chest ached, but Darius ran harder. He burst into the courtyard, eyes fixed on the gray double-doors ahead. *Almost there, almost th –* OUCH!

Darius reeled sideways as a cold wet blast rocked the right side of his face. He hit the front step off-balance, tripped, and tumbled headlong into a snowy drift of coarse bushes. He stared at the sky. From nearby, the sound of cruel laughter reached his ears.

The familiar and terrifying face of Ralph Harris leered into Darius's view. Ralph, the school's number one bully. "Whatcha doin' down there, loser?" Ralph sneered.

The school bell rang. Darius wanted to get up and run inside, into the warmth and safety of seventh grade. Instead, he lay still, waiting. *It will be over soon. Ralph has to go to school too.*

"What's the matter, Darius Dorkus? Did that snowball go in your mouth? Here, let me help you get it out." A heavy fist lowered itself in the direction of Darius's face. It connected with a *POP*, and was quickly followed by the other fist slamming into the other side of his face. Hot tears sprang to his eyes as Darius cried out in pain.

"Oops. Did I hit you too hard, Darius? I'm sorry. This'll help." The fists grabbed his coat and Darius was rolled over roughly, his face smashed into the snow. After a few more jabs to his ribs, Darius heard Ralph's footsteps crunching toward the front door. "I'll see you at lunchtime, Dorkus."

Darius lay with his face half buried in snow, letting the cold numb the twin pains on either side of his jaw. After a moment, he sniffed and cleaned his face as best he could. Darius stumbled up the stairs to the entrance, praying for a cough or sneeze to begin. Anything to send him home before lunch.

*

Ralph Harris had been tormenting Darius since the first day of school, when he stopped by Darius's lunch table and proceeded to upend a carton of cold milk into his lap. Miscellaneous pranks, insults, and embarrassments had followed. Darius weathered these minor annoyances. Milk stains washed out, after all, and shame doesn't last forever. He figured that if he ignored Ralph, the bully would grow tired and direct his attentions elsewhere. Not long after, however, the beatings had begun.

Darius didn't see a way out of the situation. Ralph threatened dire consequences should he mention the beatings to a teacher. The other students barely knew Darius existed. They didn't understand him. No one played wizards and dragons with him. No one read comic books or played video games alongside him. He thought about telling his parents, but couldn't bring himself to do it. His father would get angry. His mother would worry. They would tell the school for sure, and Darius would find Ralph waiting for him down one hallway or another.

So he bore the beatings with all the dignity and courage he could muster. He tried not to cry. He tried to ruin it for Ralph, to make him lose interest. But it was getting harder to ignore the pain and embarrassment. It was getting more and more difficult to not cry. Ralph was ruining Darius's life. How would he ever make friends? He wouldn't play wizards and dragons with someone who was constantly getting pulverized either. But what could he do?

Darius walked into a classroom full of staring faces. The teacher yelled at him for being late *yet again*. A call would be made to his parents, she said, to discuss your constant tardiness and sullen attitude. Darius wanted to tell her about Ralph. But there, in the front row, sat the bully, a wicked grin contorting his features. So Darius hung his head, mumbled apologies, and slunk to his desk.

*

Darius could barely bring himself to eat the lunch in front of him. His sandwich lay untouched. Darius tapped the table with one chewed fingernail and glanced at the clock. *Seven minutes to go.* Perhaps Ralph had forgotten. Perhaps he had gone home sick. Perhaps –

A thick fist clubbed onto the table, smashing Darius's sandwich and making him jump in alarm. His eyes shot up to view the towering form and evil eyes he'd been dreading since this morning.

"Dorkus. Sorry, I didn't see your sandwich there. It's still good, though. See?" Darius flinched as Ralph shoved the mangled peanut butter and jelly toward his face. "That's not very nice, Dorkus. Didn't your mommy make this for you? You should EAT IT!" With those words, Ralph smashed the sandwich into Darius's mouth, pushing hard. The force of the blow sent his chair tipping backwards, and Darius crashed to the cold tile floor. Ralph followed him down, fingers poking and prodding the sandwich into Darius's mouth, one lump at a time. Darius spluttered, gagged, and coughed, struggling to breathe through his nose. His legs kicked feebly under the enormous weight of Ralph. He heard laughter as the rest of the students looked on at his humiliation. Try as he might, he could not stop it. Something hot and urgent blossomed in his head, and he felt a fire burning in his chest. He struggled harder.

Mercy arrived at the sound of the bell. Sounds of commotion rose as the students hurried to their classes. The weight on his body lifted as Ralph stood, giggling, and turned to leave. Darius saw him retreating through a blur of tears. Spitting chunks of wet peanut butter and bread out of his mouth, he stumbled to his feet. His whole body felt hot. He wanted to scream. He wanted to do something to let the fire out. He watched as Ralph swaggered through the cafeteria doors.

"Pick up that chair, young man." Darius turned at the sound of the cafeteria worker's voice. He frowned at Darius and turned back to wiping the tables.

Darius picked up the chair. But instead of setting it back down, he carried it towards the door. He gripped it tight in his fingers until his knuckles turned white. No one watched him. No one stopped him. No one cared. They never did. Ralph's wide back grew closer as Darius broke into a trot. He must have heard him, because he turned around at the last second. His eyes went wide. His mouth opened to cry out. His hand rose in front of him. But he was too late.

It took two teachers and the janitor to finally wrestle Darius away from Ralph, but not before he landed several blows with the chair and his fists. Ralph was crying loudly, screaming for help. Another teacher was trying to calm him down. Students stared in shock and amazement, frozen at their lockers and at classroom doors.

Darius felt the fire inside him dwindle as he realized what he had done. The teachers turned hard eyes on him as they marched him to the Principal's office. By the time his parents were called and on their way, the fire had turned to ice.

Point of View

Discussion Questions

1. What *has* Darius done? What are the possible repercussions of his decision? Can anything positive come from his reaction? What do you think will happen next?

2. What feelings or emotions would you describe as *hot* and *cold*? Explain your answers.

3. Did Darius do a good thing? Why or why not? What else might he have done to solve his problem with Ralph?

4. If you were Darius, how would you have handled the situation?

5. At the end of the story, who is more at fault – Ralph or Darius? Give reasons to support your opinion.

6. Is it ever acceptable to use violence to solve a problem? Why or why not?

7. Why do you think bullies bully? Do you have a bullying situation at your school? What can you do to avoid or help people like Ralph?

Improvisation

Role-Playing Variations

1. Act out a conference (that takes place after the cafeteria incident) between Darius, the principal, his teacher, and Darius's parents. Darius should explain his reasons for behaving in the way he did. The principal and teacher should discuss punishments or policy changes that result from the fight. The parents should react to this shocking news of their son and side with either the school or Darius. For added roles, Ralph and his parents can be included in the conference.

2. Reinterpret the cafeteria/hallway scene from the end of the story. Students should act out more appropriate reactions to Ralph's attack.

3. Act out a local newscast's coverage of the dramatic cafeteria episode. Assign students the roles of news anchor, reporter, and key players (Darius, Ralph, student-created characters in the cafeteria, the cafeteria worker, etc.). Include interviews with the characters and reactions from various students, teachers, and parents.

4. Pair students and instruct them to improvise a scene in which Darius and Ralph sit down and calmly discuss their differences. Ralph should explain his reasons for tormenting Darius, and Darius should reveal how the bullying makes him feel. The two should also discuss a better way to handle their problems with one another, and forge a plan to get along in the future. You might have students perform their improvisations in front of the class, following each with a discussion.

Writing Suggestions

1. Imagine that you are Darius. You have decided to secretly inform your teacher about Ralph's bullying. Write a letter in which you explain the situation and your feelings about it. Next, put yourself in the teacher's position and write a response in which you detail how the situation will be handled.

2. Write a journal entry from Ralph's point of view after the incident outside the cafeteria. React to Darius's lashing out. Reflect on your treatment of him in the past. Do you feel different about him now? Have you learned a lesson? What are you going to do about all this?

3. Write a developed argument against bullying. List several reasons that discuss its negative impact on society and individuals. Back these reasons with evidence. You are trying to convince a reader that bullying must stop, so use strong and convincing language.

4. Write an alternate ending to the story. How do events unfold differently? How do these differences change the impact on each character?

Name _____   Date _____

Student Comment

An ancient adage has it that, when we are confronted, we should 'turn the other cheek.' By the end of the story, Darius completely disregards that advice. What exactly does it mean to 'turn the other cheek'? In a situation such as Darius's, how would this strategy work? Could it solve the problem of bullying? How have you 'turned the other cheek' in your life?

_____
_____
_____
_____
_____
_____
_____
_____
_____
_____
_____
_____
_____
_____
_____
_____
_____
_____
_____
_____

A Sleepless Night

Stacey cannot sleep. She tosses and she turns, flips her pillow over, counts sheep; nothing works. She rolls over and checks the clock on her dresser. It's well after midnight.

She knows why she can't sleep. Today marks the first day of high school. She is nervous, excited, and terrified all at once. She doesn't know what to expect or how to act. She is a body of confusion. So she thinks instead, and her mind won't stop spinning in circles.

Her family moved to the city after Stacey finished middle school so that her father could start a better job. The small town they had left behind had been Stacey's home since birth. All she knew was back there: her friends, her extended family, her idea of home. She'd spent most of the summer hiding in her room, reading books and writing poems. Starting tomorrow, she could hide no more.

Would she be able to make new friends? Would she like her teachers? Would the boys notice her? She shuts her eyes against the questions with no easy answers. But sleep will not come.

Sighing, Stacey flips the blankets away and climbs out of bed. A cold glass of milk will settle her down. Perhaps she'll read for a while so that her mind can focus on something other than eight o'clock. As she walks through the living room to the kitchen, she hears voices from the den. Her parents are up late. She walks across the cold floor on tiptoes, not wanting to disturb them.

"I don't know how else to handle it," Her father is speaking in low tones. "It's not perfect, but I think it's the best option."

Stacey pauses at the fridge, curious. She cocks her head to better hear her mother's reply.

"I suppose you're right," She says in a tired voice. It has an unsteady edge to it. "It's just…It's not how I expected to live my life."

"No one expects these kinds of obstacles," Her father takes a deep breath. "I could never have imagined that our marriage would fall apart."

Stacey's head goes light and the kitchen tilts unsteadily around her. She reaches out to grip the silver handle of the fridge.

"If we had figured this out before the kids were born, we might have been able to…" Her father trails off. "But a divorce now would turn their world upside down. We can't do that to them."

Stacey's breathing feels heavy and ragged. Her eyes sting at the words being spoken by her parents. All is silent for a moment.

"You're right. It's unavoidable. Stacey's had such a difficult time adjusting to the city." A pause as Stacey's mother takes a drink of something. "To throw something like this at her could lead to…complications."

"That's right," Her father responds in a sad but determined voice. "The next year could define the future for Stacey. And Zachary needs a strong example from his older sister. We've heard the horror stories about teenagers with divorced parents. We can't risk that happening to our children."

"So we figure out a way to move on," Her mother says. "We stay together for them. We get them through high school and college. Then, when they're ready to take on the world, we can figure out what's best for us."

"Who knows?" Her father's voice is heavy with false hope. "We might rediscover what drew us together in the first place."

Stacey's mother takes another drink. "Face it, dear. We're shutting the door on our own happiness and love. We do this for them. Not us – we're not important anymore."

The den falls back into silence. The tears run freely down Stacey's cheeks and drop from her chin to patter on the floor. She slowly backs out of the kitchen, through the living room, and back into the darkness of her bedroom. She smothers her sobs in the pillows and wraps herself in the blankets.

When she is able, she asks herself why she is so upset. Her parents are staying together, after all. She won't have to go through the difficulties of high school without her mother or father. She won't be one of the kids splitting time between two houses, living two different lives. She can escape the horrors of freshman year at a dinner table with her family – every member of it. She should be thankful for this.

But her mind keeps bringing back her mother's verdict: *We're shutting the door on our own happiness.* She loves her mother's smile. She adores her father's laugh. If things were really as bad between them as they seemed, would Stacey ever hear her father laugh; see her mother smile? Would things get bad? An image of a dinner table surrounded by arguments and anger comes to her. What would that environment do to her? What would it do to Zachary?

It is nearing sunrise when Stacey realizes that she has a choice to make. She can pretend that she never overheard her parents. She can go along with the charade, an actor in a play about love and family. By doing so, she can ensure that she has a united family to come home to, that Zachary won't grow up in a broken home. And she can probably be happy.

Or she can tell her mother and father that she heard. She can tell them that their happiness is important, too, assure them that she can handle the difficult times ahead. She can take care of Zachary, help him through the divorce. Together, the family can figure out how best to move forward so that everyone is happy. Stacey has the power to do this. The problem is, she isn't sure that she can.

Her alarm goes off at six-thirty, a sad song playing on the radio. Stacey rises from her bed and prepares to begin the first day of the rest of her life. What that life will be, she realizes, is up to her.

Discussion Questions

1. What do you think Stacey will do? What details in the story make you believe this? What would you do in this situation? Explain your answer.

2. How might a separation or divorce be difficult for a family? How might it be especially difficult for children? Are children of divorced parents at any sort of disadvantage? If you have experienced a divorce in your family, how did you respond? If not, how do you think such an event would impact you?

3. Why do you think Stacey's parents chose this course of action?

4. Divorce rates are much higher now than in the past. Why do you think this is? How important is love in today's world? Explain your answers.

5. Have you ever done something that you did not want to for the sake of someone that you care about? Why did you do it? Did you regret your choice later? Why or why not?

Role-Playing Variations

1. Act out the story as is appears. You can use the written lines of dialogue or adapt them to your own style.

2. Create and act out a scene in which Stacey confronts her parents about the conversation she overheard. How do her parents react? Does the confrontation change their decision? Let the actors portraying Stacey's parents discuss and decide for themselves.

3. Act out Stacey's first day of school. One student should play Stacey; the rest should portray students and teachers. Instruct actors and actresses to behave in different ways: some should be gracious and accepting, others uncaring, and the rest rude. Let the student playing Stacey choose his or her own reactions to each of the student/teacher characters. Give several students an opportunity to play Stacey. Males can play Zachary and perform the same scenario.

Writing Suggestions

1. Write the next scene to this story. What does Stacey do? How does she do it? What are the results of her actions? Give the story a clear conclusion.

2. The story states that Stacey writes poems. Write a poem, from the point of view of Stacey, about the difficult situation she finds herself in.

3. Write a letter from Stacey and Zachary's parents, to be delivered to their children when they graduate college. The letter should explain the situation that has been maintained since the discussion Stacey overheard, giving reasons for why they maintained their marriage despite its breakdown. Include how they feel about their decisions after years of living with its consequences, good and bad.

4. Write a scene of dialogue between Stacey and Zachary in which she explains their parents' difficulties to him. Reveal Zachary's character through his reactions and responses. Develop the relationship between brother and sister through their exchanges.

Name _____   Date _____

Student Comment

Stacey's parents believe that they are making the *right* decision. Are they making a *good* decision? Explain your answer. What is the difference between a good decision and a right decision, in this case and in others? Provide specific examples to support your ideas.

The Fragile Truth

Garret dunked the mop into the bucket. He swirled it around and watched the clear water cloud with filth. This was humiliating. Four months he had been working at *Chez Pasta*, the finest Italian restaurant in town. In those four short months, Garret had fallen all the way to the bottommost rung of the employee ladder.

Garret was clumsy, you see. Very clumsy. He was hired as a waiter, a difficult position for a clumsy person. Within minutes of starting a shift, his white shirt was flecked with spaghetti sauce, his shiny black shoes spattered with strands of linguini. His manager Terrence had overlooked this, but when he tripped and flung a tray stacked with plates of fettuccini alfredo onto the laps of several patrons, Garret had to be demoted.

As a host, Garret had survived almost two months. He could carry menus and lead customers to their seats without too much difficulty, as long as he didn't talk too much. He was as clumsy with words as he was with everything else, though, and it caused trouble in the end. When he jokingly greeted the restaurant's owner as 'fat cat,' (he thought it was a flattering term for someone important; *Chez Pasta*'s rather rotund owner had strongly disagreed) Terrence decided it would be best to keep Garret out of sight, in the kitchen. So he was demoted to dishwasher.

The glasses were actually made of glass, however, and now Garret found himself in the lowest of low jobs at the restaurant – kitchen cleaner. Terrence had explained how patient he was being, but that his patience was nearly gone. If Garret couldn't handle mopping the kitchen floor and wiping down the counters after each shift, he would have to go. For good. So for the past few weeks, Garret had been the most careful cleaner ever.

He was also the most bored. He knew every tile of the floor, every imperfection in the stainless steel counters. His shoulders were sore from constantly dipping and swirling, wringing and mopping.

Garret finished mopping the last corner of the kitchen and wheeled the bucket towards the supply closet. While rinsing out the bucket, an idea struck him. He and Terrence were the only people in the restaurant. If he mopped the main floor of the restaurant tonight, Terrence would notice before he left for the night. That would get him back washing dishes for sure! Mind made up, Garret refilled the bucket with clean water and headed for the dining room.

He worked quickly, arms moving the mop back and forth mechanically. Garret felt great about himself. The promotion was his for sure. He could already feel the scalding water and smell the dish soap. He lost himself thinking about working his way back to waiter.

A loud crack startled Garret from his thoughts. He looked up as multiple cracks answered the first, coming faster and faster. He turned around just in time to watch the restaurant's front window shatter into a thousand shiny pieces. He looked to the mop in his hands and realized what he'd done. He had been so focused on thoughts of promotion that he hadn't noticed how close he was to the glass. He had put the mop right through the window!

"Garret! What have you done?" Terrence stared at him from across the dining room, eyes brimming with confusion and anger.

"I – I…" Garret stuttered, mind racing. "I was mopping the dining room. I heard a crash behind me. I saw a couple kids running down the street. I think they were carrying a baseball bat." The lie flew out of his mouth before he thought to stop it.

Strangely, it didn't take much explaining to convince Terrence that Garret was telling the truth. Apparently, vandals had been damaging and destroying property in this area for months. It was likely the same people, Terrence told him as he dialed the police. Garret had a hollow feeling in his stomach, but it was too late. He couldn't tell the truth now.

A few minutes later, a black-and-white police cruiser pulled up in front of the restaurant. Garret watched as two officers stepped out of the car and eyed the shattered window. One barked something into his radio as the other approached Garret and Terrence.

He fought to control his breathing as Terrence explained the situation. The officer nodded grimly, looking at Garret every few seconds. Garret smiled weakly and stared down at the scuff marks on his shoes.

"You saw the people that did this, then?" Garret looked up to find the officer scrutinizing him, hands on his hips. "Can you describe them to me? Which way did they go?"

Garret was about to point down the street when flashing lights pulled his attention in the other direction. Another police car roared up to the curb. A third officer climbed out of the driver's side, a satisfied smirk on his face.

"I've got two kids in the back." He jerked his thumb over his shoulder as he walked. "They were snooping around Sal's Record Store two blocks over. They tried to run, but we got 'em."

Terrence took a deep, satisfied breath. The first officer looked to Garret. "Mind identifying these kids as the ones that did this?" He indicated the broken glass littering the sidewalk. The newly arrived officer was helping a young boy out of his cruiser. His hands were bound behind his back, and his eyes were wide with fear. Another boy came out next, even younger than the first.

Garret tried to speak, but his mouth had gone dry. He desperately wanted to say yes. He had to. But what if these were the wrong people? What if they were innocent kids? Then again, the police had said that there were real vandals terrorizing the neighborhood. Maybe this was all a freak coincidence, a sign that Garret's luck was changing. Maybe these were the real vandals, in which case they should go to jail for all of the property they had destroyed. Garret felt like he was split in two: keep lying, save his job and maybe get some rotten kids in trouble? Or tell the truth, get fired for sure and maybe wind up in big trouble himself for lying to the police?

Garret hadn't intended for any of this to happen. He had made a mistake and told a little lie to save his job. That was bad enough, but now someone had been arrested!

Terrence cleared his throat and frowned down at Garret. He placed a reassuring hand on his shoulder. "Go on. Tell the truth."

Point of View

Discussion Questions

1. What do you think Garret did? Did he tell the truth or lie? What would you do in his situation? Explain your answers.

2. If he chooses to lie, what are some possible negative consequences? Could there be negative consequences if he tells the truth?

3. If you were Terrence, and Garret admitted to lying about the window, what would you do? Why?

4. Have you ever tried to fix a difficult situation by telling a lie? Explain the situation and your reasons for lying. How did things turn out? Would you do things differently now?

5. Why is truth important? List specific examples of how truth helps make the world a better place.

Role-Playing Variations

1. Act out the story as it is written, but let students improvise the ending. Fill the roles of all characters, or let students create a few of their own. Discuss the class's interpretation of the story's conclusion.

2. Divide the class into small groups. Let each group create a scene in which they act out one of Garret's clumsy moments, such as the time he called the owner a 'fat cat.' Encourage them to embrace the comedy of these moments.

3. Imagine that Garret admitted to lying, and was fired from the restaurant as a result. Explain to the class that you are a manager at a different restaurant, and they are to assume the role of Garret, trying to get a new job at your business. Ask random students questions about their last job, and discuss how each student responds.

4. Let your class create a short play in which a main character has to choose between lies and the truth. Students should write a screenplay, design sets and costumes, and fill all roles. Act out the play in front of parents or other students and teachers.

Writing Suggestions

1. Write two lists. The first should be the pros of telling the truth in Garret's situation. The second should list the cons of doing so. Compare the lists. Which decision seems to be the best? Why?

2. Assume that Garret tells the truth, but is fired for his first lie. Write a letter of apology to Terrence from Garret's point of view. Try to explain why you lied about the window, and why you changed your mind and told the truth.

3. Imagine that Garret lied, but the truth was eventually discovered by the police. Write a letter of apology from Garret to the two kids that took the blame for his mistake.

4. Write a poem about the importance of truth.

5. Write a diary entry from the perspective of one of the kids accused of Garret's mistake. Explain how the story of that night ended. Talk about yourself – were you up to no good? Are you one of the vandals? Or were you just in the wrong place at the wrong time? How did the events at the restaurant make you feel?

Name _____ Date _____

Student Comment

'White lies' are untruths supposedly told for good reasons. Do they exist? If so, what are some examples of white lies? If not, why is it never acceptable to tell a lie, even if doing so accomplishes something good? Explain your answers.

_____
_____
_____
_____
_____
_____
_____
_____
_____
_____
_____
_____
_____
_____
_____
_____
_____
_____
_____
_____
_____
_____
_____

The Grime

The village of Tree Fell rises on the fringe of Grimloch Forest. It is a small settlement of log houses and straw huts, with less than a hundred inhabitants sheltered within its walls. The villagers are hard-working men and women. They trust only in one another, and fear outsiders and strangers.

The people of Tree Fell are especially wary of the Grime, the people that live deep within the forest. The Grime are covered in patches of moss, and their skin is rough as tree bark. The Grime were once believed to be monsters that ate children that strayed too far in the forest. A hundred years ago, the Grime had ventured out of the forest. It was discovered that they were a people much like the Tree Fellers. They had tried to form an alliance with the elders of Tree Fell, but they were laughed at for their mossy skin and chased from the village. Since that time, the Grime rarely leave the forest.

Once upon a time, a young Tree Feller by the name of Zanth was playing Sticks and Stones with a group of village children. The sun was bright in a blue sky and the afternoon was warm. A boy named Yalto lobbed a stone well outside the lines of play and Zanth ran to retrieve it.

The stone had landed ten strides from the forest, and Zanth eyed the shadowed foliage with wary eyes as he approached. He stooped to collect the stone and was surprised by a rustling to his right. A round, polished ball of wood bounced from the forest and rolled down the hill, where it came to rest near the other children. They gathered around it, curious and cautious.

Suddenly, out of the forest stepped a creature from bedtime stories. It was short and covered in patches of bright green moss. Dark eyes set in a face of bark stared at Zanth through strands of hair that streamed water. *A Grime.*

Zanth had never seen a Grime. He could barely move, and the stone shook in his hands.

"Hello!" The Grime spoke in a lilting voice like birdsong. "I am Oak Bole. I have lost my Cedar ball. Have you seen it?"

Before he could think of what to say or do, a large stone sailed a foot away from the Grime's face. Oak Bole flinched back and looked down the hill. The creature's sudden appearance had sent half of the players running for the safety of the village. The braver and larger Tree Feller children were walking slowly up the hill, stones hefted before them menacingly.

As more stones flew, Oak Bole yelped and scampered back into the forest, where he quickly disappeared. The village boys hung around for a few moments, calling the Grime rude names and threatening to come after him. But, of course, none of them did. After a while, the rest of the villagers turned back. Zanth moved to join them.

"Pssst," A hiss from the trees brought Zanth back around. A pair of gloomy eyes peered from behind a tree. "Nice Tree Feller. Please, will you fetch me my Cedar ball? I shall give you a gift of the forest in thanks." The thing appeared to be trembling.

Zanth turned and saw a few villagers holding back, beckoning for him to catch up. He turned and hurled the stone in his hands as hard as he could. It smashed the trunk behind which the Grime was hiding, but the boy of the forest was already gone.

*

A few days later, Zanth was picking mushrooms. As he picked, Zanth noticed the Cedar ball sitting in the grass several feet away. He approached the sphere and picked it up. It was surprisingly light. It was covered in intricate drawings and symbols that he couldn't understand. He wondered what it was used for and how it was made. Then he thought of his stone smashing into the tree trunk.

A snapping of branches caught his attention. He scanned the edge of the forest, fearing that the Grime named Oak Bole had returned for his ball. He saw nothing. He quickened his pace, moving as fast as he could to fill his basket with mushrooms. Before long, however, he heard the sound of leaves rustling. It sounded like it was coming…from right above him!

A massive weight landed on Zanth's back and brought him crashing to the ground. He rolled down the hill, coming to a stop in a scattering of mushrooms. Standing a few feet away was a giant Wood Wolf, all shining sharp teeth and bristly fur. They rarely came out of the forest, but when they did, it meant trouble for any Tree Feller caught outside the village walls. Too late, the town watchtower's bell began to ring.

The Wood Wolf padded toward Zanth, thick saliva dripping from its mouth. Zanth prepared to be devoured.

Just before it snapped its jaws shut, an object smashed into the wolf's head, knocking it sideways. A round object rolled to a stop next to Zanth. It was the Cedar ball. Its pictures and symbols were glowing a bright green. As he stared, the ball lifted into the air, spinning slowly, green light leaking from it.

The Wood Wolf stumbled unsteadily towards Zanth, eyes glazed. The ball spun faster and faster. The green light became a blurred beam shining in all directions. Suddenly, the ball flew towards the Wood Wolf. The impact caused an explosion of green light. After the brightness faded, Zanth watched the wolf running away as fast as it could for the forest. He was saved! The ball continued to float in midair. Slowly, it began to move back towards the forest.

Zanth heard the sounds of approaching feet. A handful of village guards were running his way, swords and spears catching the sunlight as they moved about. He looked to the forest, following the movement of the ball. There, at the forest's edge, stood Oak Bole, his arms outstretched as if he wanted to embrace the ball. His eyes were glowing green and his wet hair stood straight up. The patches of moss were smoking.

"Thank you, Tree Feller, for returning Oak Bole's Cedar ball. As promised, I give you gift of forest. I give you gift of life. I will speak with Wood Wolves. They listen to Grime. They shall not trouble your village again." The Grime spread his lips in a wide grin, revealing bright teeth.

Zanth stared at Oak Bole as he took the Cedar ball into his hands. "Thank you, Oak Bole."

The guards ran past Zanth, shouting at the Grime. Zanth watched them pass, concerned for his savior's safety. He looked to the forest's edge, but the boy of the forest was already gone.

TLC10596

Discussion Questions

1. In your opinion, what is the most important lesson that should be taken from this story? Discuss why that lesson is important in modern society. How can you learn from this lesson and apply it in your daily life?

2. The Grime are discriminated against by the Tree Fellers. Provide specific examples of this fact from the story. Discuss examples of discrimination throughout history. How are the experiences of the Grime similar? How are they different? Are there modern people, groups, or situations that can be compared to the Grime?

3. In your own words, describe why you think Zanth threw the rock at Oak Bole. What would you have done in Zanth's shoes? Explain your answer.

4. Despite Zanth's mistreatment of him, Oak Bole still helped him in a time of need. Imagine that you are a Grime like Oak Bole. What emotions would you feel about the Tree Fellers? How would you react to someone throwing rocks at you or insulting you? Would you have saved Zanth from the Wood Wolf? Provide reasons for each of your answers.

5. Why do you think the Tree Fellers treated the Grime so unfairly? Name some actions Tree Fellers like Zanth could perform to help ease the tensions between the two groups. Do you think these actions would be able to help fix their relationship?

Role-Playing Variations

1. Reenact the very first meeting between the Grime and the Tree Fellers. Assign half of the class roles as Grime; the second half should be Tree Fellers. Let students act out their own interpretation of how things went wrong, or try assigning specific scenarios (for example, a unique Grime custom of greeting is misinterpreted by the Tree Fellers, who become angry or afraid).

2. Divide the class into pairs. One member of each pair should assume the role of Oak Bole; the second should assume the role of Zanth. Give pairs time to create a short scene in which Zanth and Oak Bole meet again after the incident with the Wood Wolf. Have the pairs act out their scenes for the rest of the class. Briefly discuss the highlights of each presentation.

3. Instruct the class to imagine that they are the members of the Grime village. They are meeting to discuss the problems with the Tree Fellers, and to decide on the best course of action to solve them. Stress that students should approach the discussion and decisions from a Grime's point of view. Let students come up with several options. Then have them vote for a final decision. After the role-play, discuss the process, along with how students feel about the outcome. How would the class's decision impact the future?

4. After the incident with the Wood Wolf, the mayor of Tree Fell leads a group of villagers into the forest to thank the Grime for their assistance. Pick students to fill the roles of the mayor, Zanth, Zanth's parents, and student-created villagers. Let others play Oak Bole and other Grime. Encourage students to use the information provided in the story to inspire their performances.

Writing Suggestions

1. Write an account of this story's events from Oak Bole's perspective. What is he doing when he loses his Cedar ball? How does he react to the Tree Fellers' malice? What makes him decide to save Zanth from the Wood Wolf?

2. Write a travel guide to the Grime's home in Grimloch Forest. What does it look like? What do the Grime do on a typical day? What is there to do for entertainment? Be as descriptive as possible.

3. Oak Bole uses some form of power in his Cedar ball to save Zanth from the Wood Wolf. Write a description of this power. Where does it come from? How does it work? How do the Grime use it to help them? Create some original uses for the Cedar ball.

4. Create your own unique species of people or animal, like the Grime or Wood Wolves. Describe your creation's appearance, habitat, and way of life. Use your imagination!

5. Write a story that takes the themes of *The Grime* and applies them to the real world. In what ways do prejudice and discrimination take place in reality? How do your characters experience them? How do they respond?

Name _____ Date _____

Student Comment

In the story, Zanth had difficulty 'going against the crowd.' The other Tree Fellers seemed to dislike the Grime, and Zanth was unable to act differently when he encountered Oak Bole. Have you experienced something like this situation in your life? Why is it sometimes hard to do the right thing when everyone around you does the wrong thing? Which course of action holds more reward in the long run?

_____
_____
_____
_____
_____
_____
_____
_____
_____
_____
_____
_____
_____
_____
_____
_____
_____
_____
_____
_____

One to Save

Lee fastened the last straps on her life vest and tightened her helmet. She grabbed her paddle from the pile and followed her mother and sister down the bank to the river's edge. The water was calm, the first blue and red rafts drifting out into the gentle current.

Her father was waiting with the Kim family's raft. He smiled at Lee as he pulled on a waterproof shoe. He cut quite a figure in his top-of-the-line wetsuit and official rafting gear. He had been a part-time river guide for the last decade, and had rafted the rivers of the world all his life. Lee was glad she and her sister had him along for their first boating experience. And not just for his rafting skills. Dad was a gentle and loving parent. He was quick with a smile and he would do anything he could to help his family through a tight spot. He also happened to be incredibly funny and goofy. He could have his wife and daughters rolling on the floor laughing in no time.

Her mother had argued that her little sister was too young, but Ming and Dad had teamed up against her. Ming was only in second grade, but she had a strong spirit and never gave up on anything. Lee smiled as she remembered her sister's determined frown during the debate.

Mother had been on a raft exactly once before – the first time Dad had taken her out, before the girls were born. She had sworn never to set foot on raft ever again. The only reason she was coming along today was to keep an eye on the girls, or so she claimed. But Lee could see the excitement in her eyes.

Lee often referred to her mother as the brains of the parental operation. A doctor whose vocation included researching cures for disease, Mother was always trying to teach her children new things. She could handle any homework question, and she always made sure Ming and Lee understood something before they were done. Lee could also talk with Mother about anything, even some things she wasn't able to bring up with Dad – boys, fights with her best friends, fashion – Mother always had sound advice for her.

The three female Kims clambered into the small raft and took their assigned positions. Mother made sure the girls' equipment was snug and properly arranged before settling herself in. When a spot opened up in the line of rafts navigating the river, Dad pushed their raft into the shallows and hopped in. The raft slowly bobbed out to the center of the river and a few dips of their paddles directed them downstream.

She was glad to be sharing this experience with her family. Nothing was as important to her as the people sharing that small raft. The Kims were extremely close. To hear her ancient grandmother tell it, the family had been inseparable throughout history, all the way back to their origins in China. The respect for one's parents had been passed down through the generations. Sometimes, Lee's friends complained about their mothers and fathers, even made fun of them or spoke angrily about them. Lee didn't understand how they could do this.

Ming giggled as the raft gained momentum in the quickening current. Lee loved her little sister. They were inseparable. Ming was adorable and free-spirited. Whenever Lee was feeling down, she would play with her sister. Within minutes, Ming would have her smiling, and whatever problems she had would fade away. Lee knew that the two of them would be best friends for life, close even when they were old. So she made sure to watch out for Ming – at school, at home, everywhere. She would do anything to keep her safe, happy, and healthy.

The raft rounded a corner and the first rapids came into view, surges of white foam rolling in the waters. Dad calmly repeated the instructions he'd spoken over the campfire the night before. Anxiety tugged at Lee's stomach as the rapids came closer. A tiny hand gripped hers. She looked over to see Ming's wide smile. She felt better.

They handled the first rapids wonderfully. Mother cried out in delight as the boat dipped and rocked, foam splashing. They came through the end and the river calmed again. Dad laughed and congratulated his family. The next rapids, he explained, would be more difficult. Lee saw them ahead, watched the other boats bouncing through. She tightened her grip on the paddle and glanced over to make certain Ming was ready. Mother looked back and smiled at her girls.

Lee saw the floating tree trunk as Dad steered the raft into position. It was large, and it was heading straight for their raft. She started to warn Dad, but the raft had already entered the rapids. She cried out as the stump slammed into the side of the raft. The impact was strong enough to push the raft slightly off course and out of Dad's intended path. Dad flashed his paddle into the water and tried to get back on line, but the raft rolled up and raked along a rock protruding from the water's chaotic surface. A terrible tearing sound was followed by the sound of escaping air.

A shout brought Lee's head around. She watched in horror as Ming was bounced into the air by the jolt of raft against rock. Thankfully, her sister landed in the raft. But the raft was deflating quickly. It was stuck on the debris caught around the rock. Lee glimpsed the other rafts floating downriver. They couldn't help – the current was too strong!

Then she saw it. The floating tree trunk that had knocked them into the rock had lodged between two rocks. She wasn't sure, but Lee thought she might be able to reach it. She screamed at her father as he looked about for a means of escape. She pointed to the trunk. Dad calmly nodded. The raft would only last for a few more seconds. Lee was the only one that had a chance at reaching the trunk. She gathered her strength and leapt from the raft, arm outstretched…

…and splashed into the icy and surging water. Her head went under. For a moment, Lee thought she was going to be pulled beneath the surface. But her hand grasped something rough – the trunk! She pulled herself above the surface, sucking in a deep breath of air. The trunk held firm. She twisted to see her family clinging to the last part of the raft above water.

Lee knew she only had seconds. She could grab one of them with her free arm and hold on for as long as she could. Maybe she could hold on until help arrived. Time seemed to slow as Lee looked from one face to the next, dad to Ming to mother. How could she choose? The two that she couldn't hold would be pulled under. The current was strong and there were jagged rocks everywhere.

The last of the raft tore away, and Lee's family started to lurch downstream. Lee screamed in defiance and thrust her hand towards them, reaching with all her might. Her hand closed around a wrist and she held on tight.

Discussion Questions

1. Who do you think Lee chose to save? Why do you think so? What details from the story support your choice?

2. Which person would you have saved in Lee's position? Explain your answer.

3. Do you think Lee's decision is motivated by logic or by impulse? Would your decision be the same or different? Explain your answers.

4. Which family member do you think is Lee's favorite? Use specific details from the story to support your claim.

5. Could you pick between the members of your family in a situation like that in the story? Why or why not?

Improvisation

Role-Playing Variations

1. Act out the scene in which Lee chooses who to save. Give each student an opportunity to assume the role of Lee and her family members. After each actor or actress has chosen, ask him or her to explain their reasons.

2. Act out a news interview with Lee and the person she chose to save. Let the interviewer improvise the questions and Lee and her family member the answers. Let other students call out questions of their own.

3. Challenge students to create similar scenes in which a character has to choose between several very important persons or things. Students should create a cast of characters, a setting and situation, and their own lines of dialogue. Let other students volunteer to be a part of each performance, and dedicate an afternoon to watching the plays.

Writing Suggestions

1. Write the next part of the story. Who does Lee save? How do they get to shore? What happens to the other two family members? Finish your story with a clear resolution.

2. Write a newspaper article about the event. Create conclusions for each member of the family. Include interviews and witness accounts.

3. Write a scene in which Lee and her remaining family members (those you choose to survive) return to the river ten years after the incident. Describe each character's situation. How have they changed over the last decade? How did the boating accident change their lives? How do they feel coming back to the river?

Name _____ Date _____

Student Comment

Different cultures value different things. Some cultures, like the Chinese, value their elders much more highly than others, like Americans. Someone so minded may very well have chosen to save the father, out of respect for his age and wisdom. What does our culture value the most? Why do you think this is so? What do you value the most? Explain your answers.

_____
_____
_____
_____
_____
_____
_____
_____
_____
_____
_____
_____
_____
_____
_____
_____
_____
_____